WE SHALL ESCAPE THE
ABSURDITY OF GROWING
A WHOLE CHICKEN IN ORDER
TO EAT THE BREAST OR
WING, BY GROWING THESE
PARTS SEPARATELY UNDER
A SUITABLE MEDIUM.

WINSTON CHURCHILL — 1931

BISPUBLISHERS

Building Het Sieraad
Postjesweg 1
1057 DT Amsterdam
The Netherlands
T +31 (0)20 515 02 30
F +31 (0)20 515 02 39
bis@bispublishers.nl
www.bispublishers.nl

Editing and design: Koert van Mensvoort and Hendrik-Jan Grievink

ISBN 978 90 6369 358 9

Copyright © 2014 Next Nature Network and BIS Publishers.

www.bistro-invitro.com

THE
IN VITRO
MEAT
COOKBOOK

CONTENTS

1. SAVE THE PLANET

2. STOP HURTING ANIMALS

3. FEED THE WORLD

4. EXPLORE NEW FOOD CULTURES

BY KOERT VAN MENSVOORT

Hello meat lovers, hello vegetarians! We need to talk about the future of meat. With the world's population expected to reach nine billion people by 2050, it becomes impossible to produce and consume meat like we do today. Climate change, energy use, animal diseases and global food shortages are just some of the problems facing us, not to mention the issue of animal welfare on factory farms. Will we soon be limited to eating rice, beans and seaweed burgers? Insects perhaps?

Some researchers expect that in vitro meat, grown from stem cells in a bioreactor, could provide a sustainable and animal-friendly alternative to conventional meat and in 2013 the world's first lab grown burger was cooked. Nevertheless, many people still find it an unattractive idea to eat meat from a lab. And rightly so. Because before we can decide whether we will ever be willing to consume in vitro meat, we must explore the new food cultures it may bring us. Although it is tempting to think we will simply mimic the hamburgers, sausages and steaks we already have, in vitro technology also has a unique potential to bring us new food products, tools and traditions we can hardly imagine today.

This cookbook aims to move beyond in vitro meat as inferior fake-meat replacement, to explore its creative prospects and visualize what in vitro meat products might be on our plate one day. Recipes range from knitted meat, to meat fruit and meat ice cream.

The recipes are organized in four chapters, each focusing on a meat-related issue that may be addressed with in vitro meat:

1. Growing meat sustainably.
2. Avoiding harm to animals.
3. Preventing food shortages.
4. Exploration of new food cultures.

In addition to this you will find essays, interviews, and graphs that provide for background information on the technology, its history, promises, potential pitfalls and moral implications. Because in vitro meat is still in an early phase of development, it is a cookbook from which you cannot cook, just yet. The number of stars with each recipe indicates its technological feasibility. One star means that the dish is far from being realized, while five stars means it might soon go into production.

All recipes have been created by a team of chefs, designers and artists. While some dishes are innovative and delicious, others are uncanny and macabre. Our aim is not to promote lab-grown meat, nor to predict the future, but to visualize a wide range of possible new dishes and food cultures to help us decide what future we actually want. Bon appetit!

A HISTORY OF MEAT—EATING

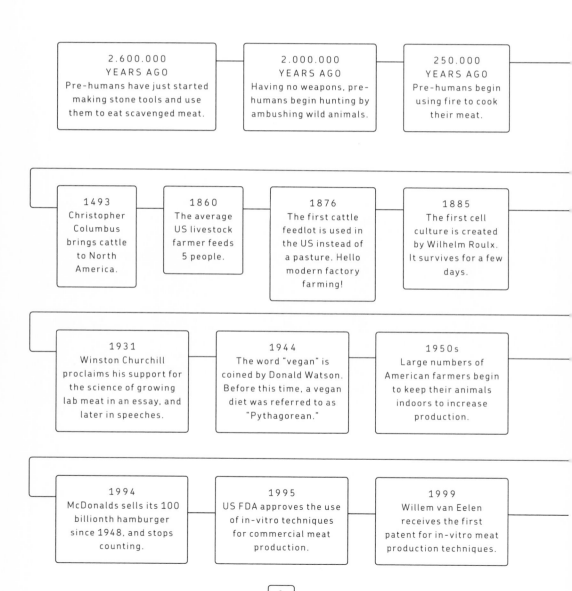

2.600.000 YEARS AGO
Pre-humans have just started making stone tools and use them to eat scavenged meat.

2.000.000 YEARS AGO
Having no weapons, pre-humans begin hunting by ambushing wild animals.

250.000 YEARS AGO
Pre-humans begin using fire to cook their meat.

1493
Christopher Columbus brings cattle to North America.

1860
The average US livestock farmer feeds 5 people.

1876
The first cattle feedlot is used in the US instead of a pasture. Hello modern factory farming!

1885
The first cell culture is created by Wilhelm Roulx. It survives for a few days.

1931
Winston Churchill proclaims his support for the science of growing lab meat in an essay, and later in speeches.

1944
The word "vegan" is coined by Donald Watson. Before this time, a vegan diet was referred to as "Pythagorean."

1950s
Large numbers of American farmers begin to keep their animals indoors to increase production.

1994
McDonalds sells its 100 billionth hamburger since 1948, and stops counting.

1995
US FDA approves the use of in-vitro techniques for commercial meat production.

1999
Willem van Eelen receives the first patent for in-vitro meat production techniques.

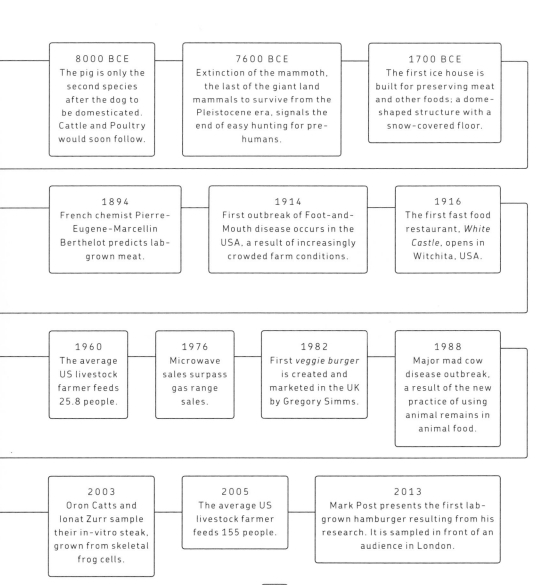

8000 BCE
The pig is only the second species after the dog to be domesticated. Cattle and Poultry would soon follow.

7600 BCE
Extinction of the mammoth, the last of the giant land mammals to survive from the Pleistocene era, signals the end of easy hunting for pre-humans.

1700 BCE
The first ice house is built for preserving meat and other foods; a dome-shaped structure with a snow-covered floor.

1894
French chemist Pierre-Eugene-Marcellin Berthelot predicts lab-grown meat.

1914
First outbreak of Foot-and-Mouth disease occurs in the USA, a result of increasingly crowded farm conditions.

1916
The first fast food restaurant, *White Castle*, opens in Witchita, USA.

1960
The average US livestock farmer feeds 25.8 people.

1976
Microwave sales surpass gas range sales.

1982
First *veggie burger* is created and marketed in the UK by Gregory Simms.

1988
Major mad cow disease outbreak, a result of the new practice of using animal remains in animal food.

2003
Oron Catts and Ionat Zurr sample their in-vitro steak, grown from skeletal frog cells.

2005
The average US livestock farmer feeds 155 people.

2013
Mark Post presents the first lab-grown hamburger resulting from his research. It is sampled in front of an audience in London.

HOW TO MAKE AN IN VITRO BURGER?

1

Harvest muscle tissue from a sedated or recently slaughtered animal. Make sure to gather muscle from an area close to the bone.

2

Using a microscope, separate out myosatellite cells from the normal muscle cells. Myosatellites are cells that are halfway between a stem cell and a fully differentiated cell. Stems cells are 'undecided' and can become anything, whereas satellites cells can only become one kind of cell. Myosatellites are found all over the body, ready to turn into adult muscle cells in case of injury. Myosatellites are particularly useful for in vitro meat, because they not only 'want' to become muscle, they're also able to rapidly proliferate – which you'll need for the next step.

3

Place each myosatellite cell in a petri dish and bathe it in a suitable nutrient solution supplemented with fetal bovine serum. Derived from the blood of unborn calves, this serum is the standard solution for growing healthy cells, although algae-based alternatives are becoming possible. After three weeks, each myosatellite cell will have produced several billion additional cells.

4

Place your cells in a nutrient poor growth medium. This essentially 'starves' the cells, forcing them to differentiate into fully developed muscle cells, also called myocytes or muscle fibers.

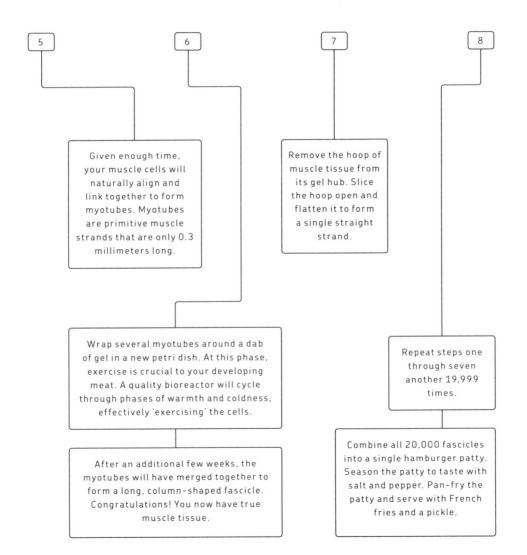

5

Given enough time, your muscle cells will naturally align and link together to form myotubes. Myotubes are primitive muscle strands that are only 0.3 millimeters long.

6

Wrap several myotubes around a dab of gel in a new petri dish. At this phase, exercise is crucial to your developing meat. A quality bioreactor will cycle through phases of warmth and coldness, effectively 'exercising' the cells.

After an additional few weeks, the myotubes will have merged together to form a long, column-shaped fascicle. Congratulations! You now have true muscle tissue.

7

Remove the hoop of muscle tissue from its gel hub. Slice the hoop open and flatten it to form a single straight strand.

8

Repeat steps one through seven another 19,999 times.

Combine all 20,000 fascicles into a single hamburger patty. Season the patty to taste with salt and pepper. Pan-fry the patty and serve with French fries and a pickle.

MEAT THE FACTS

TO MAKE A HAMBURGER OF 200 GRAM YOU NEED:

3 kilograms of grain and forage, 200 liters of water for the irrigation of land and for cattle to drink, 7 m² for grazing and growing feed crops and 1.093 kJ of fossil energy to grow and transport feed; enough to power your microwave for 18 minutes.

MEAT CONSUMPTION

The global average for meat consumption is 42 kilograms. People in the developing world eat an average of 32 kilos of meat each year, compared to 80 kilos of meat in industrialized countries. Below the meat consumption in per capita in the year 2009, according to the United Nations:

USA: 125 KG
Kuwait: 119 KG
Spain: 97 KG
The Netherlands: 85.5 KG
China: 58.2 KG
Rwanda: 6.5 KG
India: 4.4 KG

GAS EMISSIONS

The United Nations estimates that the global greenhouse gas emissions from the total supply chain of producing livestock for meat range from 15% to 18% per year. A more in-depth report from the WorldWatch Institute indicates that this number is actually closer to 51%.

ANIMALS KILLED IN THE USA

Cattle: 35,507,500
Pigs: 116,558,900
Chickens: 9,075,261,000
Layer hens: 69,683,000
Broiler chickens: 9,005,578,000
Turkeys: 271,245,000

Source: USDA statistics 2008

FOOD WASTE

30 to 50% of all food produced globally is never eaten, due to supply chain in efficiencies, crops left to rot in fields, consumers rejecting 'imperfect' foods or throwing away food after purchase.

WATER USE

Water use for in vitro meat would be 82 to 96% lower than for conventional meat*.It takes 20 to 50 times the amount of water to produce one kilo of meat than one kilo of vegetables. It takes 20 to 50 times the amount of water to produce one kilo of meat than one kilo of vegetables.

ECOLOGICAL FOOTPRINT

Between now and 2050 global livestock production is predicated to nearly double. Studies indicate that in vitro meat would require far less energy input than beef, pork or mutton, but that it would require more energy than poultry such as ducks or chickens*. Compared to conventional meat, greenhouse gas emissions for in vitro meat would be up to 96% lower*.

* These numbers assume that cyanobacteria will be the feedstock for in vitro meat, which is not yet possible.

LAND USE

66% of agricultural land is used to grow animal feed; only 8% of agricultural land goes to food that we directly consume. 30% of ice-free land on earth is used for livestock raised for meat. In vitro meat could require only 1 to 2% of the land area used to produce the same amount of conventional meat.

IN THE YEAR 2030

The global middle class will balloon from 1.8 billion today to a staggering 4.4 billion by 2030. In fact, we're almost talking about a tripling of the meat-eating class.

CALORIE SUPPLY

The Netherlands: 1,151.4 Kcal/person/day
Kuwait: 524.6 Kcal/person/day
Spain: 936.6 Kcal/person/day
China: 618 Kcal/person/day
Rwanda: 60.5 Kcal/person/day
India: 198.4 Kcal/person/day

Source: Chartsbin.com

IN THE YEAR 2050

The world's population will be 9.6 billion people by 2050, compared to 7.1 billion people as of 2013. Global meat consumption may have doubled by that time, mostly as a consequence of increasing world population, but also because of increased per capita meat consumption from 2000 to 2050.

UNKNOWN IS UNLOVED?

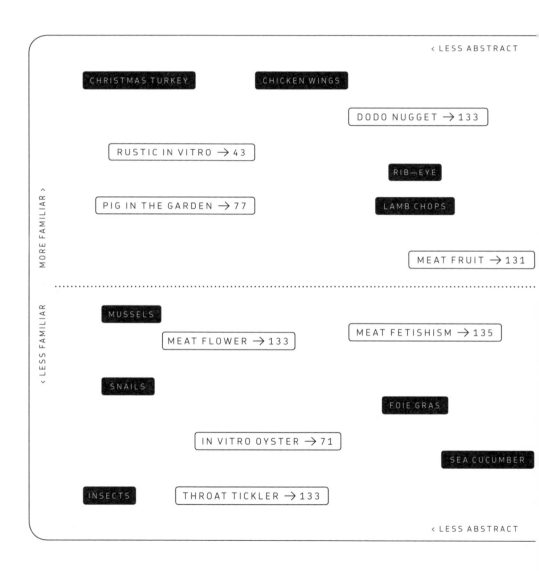

< LESS ABSTRACT

CHRISTMAS TURKEY   CHICKEN WINGS

DODO NUGGET → 133

RUSTIC IN VITRO → 43

RIB—EYE

PIG IN THE GARDEN → 77

LAMB CHOPS

MEAT FRUIT → 131

MORE FAMILIAR >

< LESS FAMILIAR

MUSSELS

MEAT FLOWER → 133   MEAT FETISHISM → 135

SNAILS

FOIE GRAS

IN VITRO OYSTER → 71

SEA CUCUMBER

INSECTS   THROAT TICKLER → 133

< LESS ABSTRACT

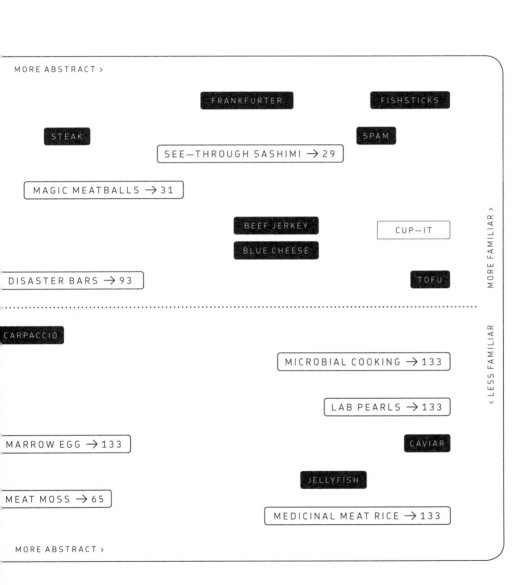

MORE ABSTRACT >

FRANKFURTER

FISHSTICKS

STEAK

SPAM

SEE—THROUGH SASHIMI → 29

MAGIC MEATBALLS → 31

BEEF JERKEY

CUP—IT

BLUE CHEESE

DISASTER BARS → 93

TOFU

MORE FAMILIAR >

CARPACCIO

MICROBIAL COOKING → 133

< LESS FAMILIAR

LAB PEARLS → 133

MARROW EGG → 133

CAVIAR

JELLYFISH

MEAT MOSS → 65

MEDICINAL MEAT RICE → 133

MORE ABSTRACT >

WHAT'S YOUR POSITION?

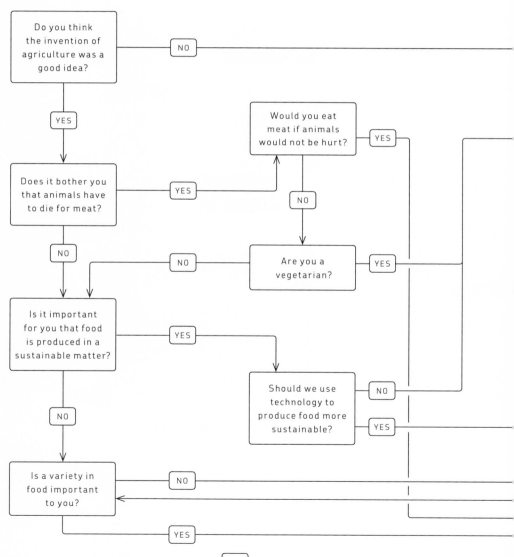

Do you think the invention of agriculture was a good idea?

NO

YES

Does it bother you that animals have to die for meat?

YES

Would you eat meat if animals would not be hurt?

YES

NO

NO

Are you a vegetarian?

YES

Is it important for you that food is produced in a sustainable matter?

YES

Should we use technology to produce food more sustainable?

NO

YES

Is a variety in food important to you?

NO

YES

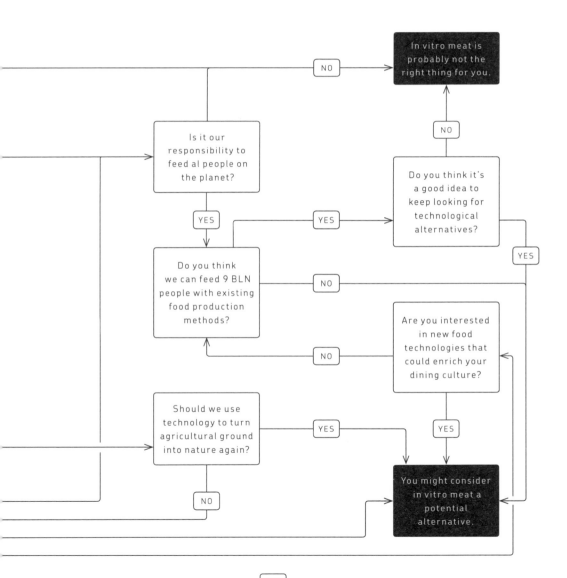

In vitro meat is probably not the right thing for you.

Is it our responsibility to feed al people on the planet?

NO

Do you think it's a good idea to keep looking for technological alternatives?

NO

YES

YES

Do you think we can feed 9 BLN people with existing food production methods?

NO

YES

Are you interested in new food technologies that could enrich your dining culture?

NO

Should we use technology to turn agricultural ground into nature again?

YES

YES

NO

You might consider in vitro meat a potential alternative.

While most people know about climate change and deforestation, it is less known that meat eating is a major factor in these environmental issues. With 66% of agricultural land used to grow animal feed, meat production can be held responsible for 39% of all emitted methane and 5% of carbon dioxide. Researchers expect in vitro meat could put a cap on the tremendous impact of the livestock industry on our environment. If in vitro meat becomes widely applied, crowded factory farms and overgrazed fields will no longer be needed. Rainforests can grow back into rangeland and even the oceans will be looking a little less empty. In vitro meat could solve a wealth of ecological issues, yet, it would bring change to our dinner plates as well.

POSTBURGER

In August 2013, Professor Mark Post unveiled the world's first hamburger made entirely from lab-grown meat. Fashioned from 20,000 strands of muscle fiber, the prototype cost a staggering €250,000 to make. As technology advances, postburgers should be so cheap that they become standard in fast food outlets around the world. Despite being blander than conventional ground beef, the Postburger's low price, safety and eco credentials could win over the food industry and consumers alike.

For nostalgic carnivores, the vibrant red juice of this 'bleeding' burger recalls the blood from a fresh kill. Between the cheese, the egg and the crunchy buttered bun, there are more than enough animal products in this rendition of the Postburger to win over even the most stubborn traditionalist.

BLEEDING BURGER

- 1 beet
- 1 slice Gouda cheese
- 1 postburger
- 1 egg
- sandwich bun, split
- 1 tablespoon butter, melted
- Vegetable oil
- Salt and pepper

① Preheat the oven to 200° C. Wrap the beet in tinfoil. Roast for one hour, until a knife meets no resistance when inserted in the center. Let the beet cool, then peel and slice.

② Change the oven to the broiler setting. Melt the butter in a small saucepan. Brush both sides of the bun with the butter, then toast in the oven for one minute. Remove to a plate.
③ Heat vegetable oil in a skillet over medium-high heat until just beginning to smoke. Season the postburger with salt and pepper and cook for two minutes. Flip the burger and top with the cheese slice. Cook for another minute.Transfer the burger to the bun.

④ Heat additional vegetable oil in the skillet. Crack the egg into the pan. Cover with a lid and cook until the egg white has just set. Top the burger with a slice of beet and the fried egg.

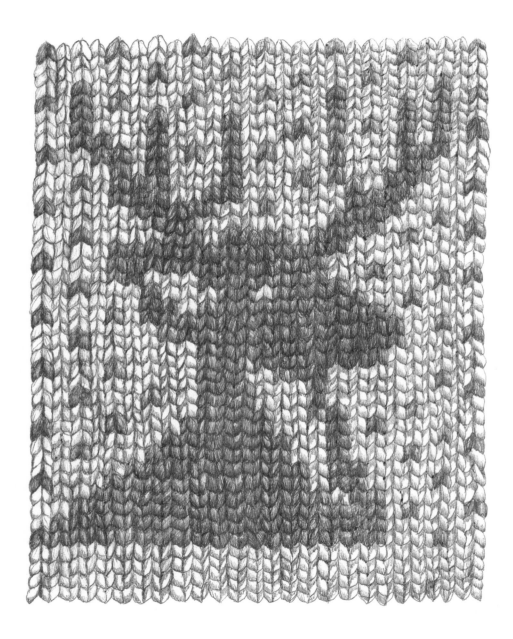

KNITTED MEAT

The length of a muscle fiber was once limited by the size of the animal it was growing in. Now, freed from the constraints of the body, it's possible to culture 'thread' made from continuing strands of muscle tissue. Colorful spools of meat yarn, from the light pink of chicken to the vibrant red of beef, can be woven into eye-catching patterns.

Supermarkets could install knitting machines with pre-set patterns, making it easy to knit a package of burgers or a meaty scarf. A portable model could come with easy-to-use design software for home knitters. Knitting enthusiasts could enjoy gathering in walk-in refrigerators to swap techniques. Over the holidays, many families could replaced the traditional turkey or ham with a festive centerpiece of Knitted Meat.

SHEPHERD'S KNITTED PIE

- 1 kilo knitted meat
- 1 kilo potatoes
- 100 milliliters milk
- 60 grams butter
- 1 large onion, diced
- 2 carrots, peeled and diced
- 2 celery stalks, diced
- 2 garlic cloves, minced
- 1 can of diced tomatoes
- 250 milliliters stock
- 1 teaspoon Worcestershire sauce

① Preheat the oven to 160° C. Boil the potatoes until cooked through. Drain and mash the potatoes with the butter and milk. Season to taste.

② While the potatoes are boiling, heat oil in a skillet and sauté the onion, garlic, celery and carrots until softened. Add the tomatoes, stock and Worcestershire sauce and simmer for 10 minutes.

③ Spread the potato mixture in a baking dish. Top with the vegetable mixture, followed by the meat. Trim the meat to fit, and season to taste. Cover the dish with tinfoil and bake for 25 minutes. Remove the tinfoil and bake another 10 minutes or until the meat is browned.

★★☆☆☆

The Home Incubator does for cooking what the electronic synthesizer did for musicians. A set of pre-programmed meats, tastes and textures allow home cooks to grow mind-boggling varieties of meat, from tuna steak to turkey meatballs, to venison sausage. Adventurous cooks could remix species and styles, making delectable new creations that push the boundaries of what it means to be meat.

The Home Incubator's website hosts lively forums where professional and amateur chefs can provide links to download what they're growing. One of the most popular recipes will surely be Everything Stew. When cooks will realize they could fit 13 kinds of bioreactor-fresh meats into a single soup, they will pounce at the chance for a carnivore's nirvana.

EVERYTHING STEW

- 3 large onions, diced
- 8 garlic cloves, minced
- 3 cans whole peeled tomatoes
- 4 bay leaves
- 4 liters vegetable stock
- 300 grams each lab-grown beef, pork, goat, duck, chicken, red snapper, grouper, lobster, mussel, clam, scallops and shrimp meat
- Vegetable oil

① In a very large stockpot, heat a generous pour of oil until just beginning to smoke. Working in batches, cook the beef, pork, goat, duck and chicken until browned on all sides. Remove the meat to a plate.

② In the remaining oil, sauté the onions and garlic until softened and fragrant. Add the tomatoes, breaking up with a wooden spoon as they cook, about seven minutes.

③ Add the beef, pork, goat, bay leaves and stock. Cover and simmer for one and a half hours. Add the chicken and duck, uncover, and simmer another half hour.

④ Add the seafood and simmer until just cooked through, about five minutes. Serve with crusty bread for mopping up the stew.

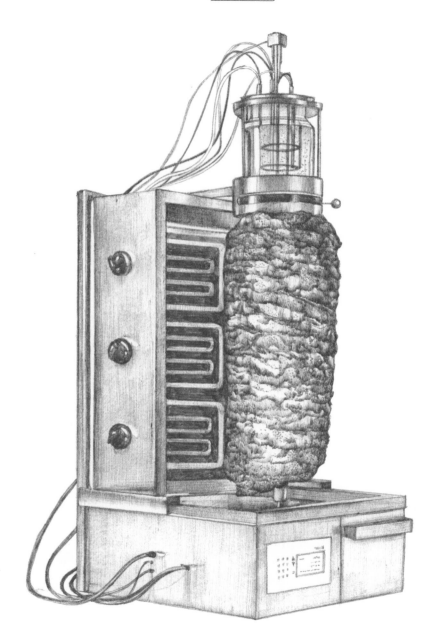

IN VITRO KEBAB

Home to a cutting-edge cell culture facility and dozens of shawarma restaurants, the Whitechapel area in London is an ideal place to introduce the world's first combination bioreactor-grill. In this device, cultured lamb is roasted as it matures, ensuring a constant supply of fresh, fat-free kebab meat. The In Vitro Kebab grill takes advantage of the fact that standard doner kebab is an abstracted tube shape — most customers won't even notice that they're eating cultured meat.

After the success of the in vitro kebab grill in Whitechapel, all 1,200 doner kebab restaurants in London could be retrofitted with the new device. Because the device produces meat that is simultaneously vegan, halal and kosher, its popularity knows no borders. In Vitro Kebab could spread throughout Europe and the Middle East.

IN VITRO KEBAB SANDWICH

- 120 milliliters tahini
- 3 cloves garlic, crushed
- 1/2 teaspoon salt
- 2 tablespoons olive oil
- 60 milliliters lemon juice
- 150 grams in vitro kebab meat
- 1 pita bread
- 1/2 tomato, diced
- 1/4 cucumber, diced
- Chopped parsley
- Crumbled feta cheese
- Shredded romaine lettuce
- Sumac

① Using a food processor or a mortar and pestle, mash the garlic and tahini into a paste. Transfer the paste to a bowl. Whisk the salt, olive oil, and lemon juice into the paste.

② To assemble the kebab sandwich: start with a generous layer of meat at the bottom of the pita, then add lettuce, tomato, cumber, parsley and feta cheese. Finish the sandwich with a drizzle of tahini sauce and a dusting of sumac.

★ ★ ★ ★ ☆

28

SEE-THROUGH SASHIMI

Without blood vessels, nerves or organs, in vitro meat can be manufactured to be nearly transparent. See-Through Sashimi mimics the same physical structures that make glass frogs look like glass or jellyfish look like jelly, creating nearly invisible meat with a pure, delicate flavor.

Grown in thin sheets in completely sterile conditions, See-Through Sashimi is cultured from meltingly tender blue fin tuna. Not only is it fattier and tastier than real tuna, it could also halt the overfishing of these threatened species. Arrange slices of see-through tuna like a traditional platter of fugu sashimi, or put a European spin on the dish by constructing a stained glass window made entirely of seafood.

SEE-THROUGH SUSHI

- 400 grams short grain Japanese rice
- 60 milliliters white wine vinegar
- 60 milliliters rice vinegar
- 50 grams sugar
- 2 tablespoons salt
- See-through tuna sashimi

① Rinse the rice five times and drain. Cook the rice in a rice cooker, or boil according to package instructions.

② Combine the two vinegars, sugar, and salt in a small saucepan. Warm until the sugar has dissolved.

③ Transfer the rice to a large bowl. Sprinkle half of the seasoned vinegar over the rice. Using a spatula or flat wooden spoon, incorporate the vinegar into the rice using a slicing motion. Take care not to mash the rice. While incorporating the rice with one hand, use a fan in the other hand to cool the rice. Add more vinegar to taste.

④ Moisten your hands in clean water. Form a ball of rice into a small log. Place the log on top of a slice of see-through sashimi. Gently roll the two together. Repeat with the remaining pieces of sushi. Serve with soy sauce and wasabi.

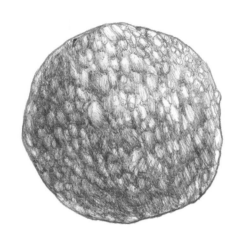

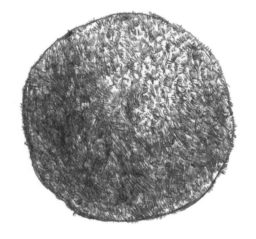

Magic Meatballs playfully familiarize children with the concept of in vitro meat. Just like modeling clay, a package of Magic Meatballs comes in a rainbow of meat colors, with exciting add-ins for flavor, texture and nutrition. Kids love to help out in the kitchen by transforming healthy in vitro meat into beach balls, Easter eggs or even pint-sized snowmen.

With the solar system activity pack, kids can create fun meatballs while learning about the planets. Use these serving suggestions to make your own tasty universe. To complete the look of an outer space expedition, serve the meatballs with black pasta and a sprinkle of 'stardust', or Parmesan cheese.

MEAT SOLAR SYSTEM

SUN
- 30 grams yellow meat
- 1 crispy-crackle pack
- 1 sunlight flavor pack

EARTH
- 15 grams blue meat
- 15 grams green meat
- 1 antioxidant flavor pack

MOON
- 30 grams white meat
- 1 pearly-sparkle pack

MARS
- 30 grams red meat
- 1 warrior flavor pack

① Mix the meat and the flavor packs in separate bowls.

② Roll the meat into balls approximately four centimeters in diameter.

③ To preserve the vibrant color of the meatballs, steam them for 10 minutes in a bamboo steamer.

A kid's version of mom and dad's countertop bioreactor, the Kid's Cooking Kit makes growing in vitro meat simple and fun for young food scientists. Each colorful bioreactor comes fully equipped with a microscope, package of nutrient serum, and a starter culture of chicken cells. A window into the bioreactor chamber lets children keep track of their meat as it develops from tiny cells into full-grown muscle fibers. After kids have mastered chicken, they could move on to more exciting meats like rainbow pony or woolly mammoth. The Kid's Cooking Kit makes the process of growing in vitro meat familiar and relatable for children.

EASY MEATY MAC'N'CHEESE

- 1 packet stem cells, any red meat
- 250 grams cooked pasta
- 2 large handfuls shredded cheddar cheese
- 240 milliliters whole milk
- 3/4 teaspoon salt
- 1/2 teaspoon black pepper
- 1 tablespoon vegetable oil

① Do ahead: grow the stem cells according to package instructions. Harvest the muscle tissue when it weighs approximately 100 grams.

② Season the meat with salt and pepper. Heat the oil in a saucepan. Cook the meat, breaking it into small pieces with a wooden spoon, until the meat is no longer raw in the center.

③ Add the pasta, cheese, and milk to the saucepan. Cook on medium heat, stirring constantly, until the cheese sauce is creamy and smooth.

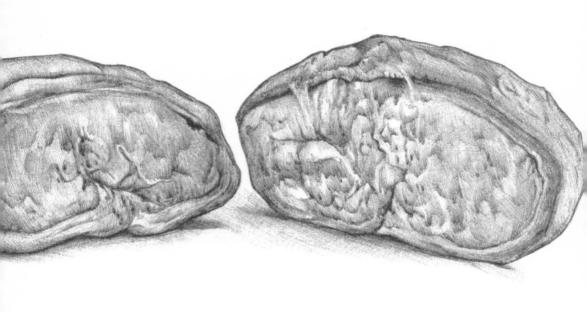

MICROBIAL COOKING

Microbial Cooking introduces an entirely new method to eat meat. While fermentation has long been used to make yoghurt, beer and cheese, it's had little application in the realm of meat. Requiring no heat and minimal electricity, the Microbial Cooking appliance uses the power of beneficial bacteria to 'cook' lab-grown meat.

Simply knead a packet of bacterial culture into a ball of ground meat, and place it in the fermentation chamber. Some bacteria, like Lactobacillus, help to cure the meat, while others, from the standard Micrococcus to more exotic genetically modified species, produce flavors from malted milk to cheese. The device regulates temperature and humidity, and prevents the growth of dangerous bacteria associated with food spoilage. Microbial Cooking allows cooks to prepare meat in a more natural way than ever possible with microwaves or electric ovens.

STEAMED BUNS

- 8 grams instant dried yeast
- 1/2 teaspoon white vinegar
- 160 milliliters lukewarm water
- 100 grams wheat starch
- 280 grams flour
- 90 grams powdered sugar
- 10 grams baking powder
- 30 grams vegetable shortening
- 10 milliliters cold water
- 250 grams microbial meat, bbq flavor

① Sift together starch, flour and sugar in a large bowl. Make a well in the center of the mixture. In a separate bowl, mix the yeast, lukewarm water, and vinegar. Pour the liquid mixture into the well in the flour. Add the shortening and knead the dough for 10 minutes, until smooth and soft. Cover the dough with a damp cloth and let rest for 30 minutes.

② Divide the dough into 16 equal portions. Using a rolling pin, flatten each ball into an eight centimeter circle. Scoop a tablespoon of the microbial meat into the center of each circle. Pleat the dough to seal it.

③ Set a bamboo steamer over a pot of boiling water. Set the buns into the steamer, and steam for 12 minutes. Remove the buns from the steamer and cool on a wire rack. Repeat with the remaining buns.

According to legend, Cleopatra dissolved a pearl in her drink in order to win a bet with Marc Anthony over who could spend the most on a meal. Nowadays, extravagant queens have it a little easier thanks to lab pearls. These delicate structures, reminiscent of fish roe or tapioca balls, are filled with lab-grown animal fat. Drop a few into your salad for a burst of flavor. Scatter some across a freshly toasted baguette with a sprinkle of gray sea salt. Lab pearls are also suitable for traditional foods. They can be used to replace the schmaltz in matzo balls or the lard in Mexican tamales. An aged variety even matches the taste of fine Italian lardo. Time to pile on the pearls!

THREE PEARL COCKTAIL

- 1 tablespoon pomegranate seeds
- 1 tablespoon lab pearls, lardo flavor
- 1 teaspoon basil seeds
- 100 milliliters of pomegranate juice
- Basil leaves, for garnish

1. Soak the basil seeds in a bowl of lukewarm water for two minutes. Drain the water.

2. Combine the pomegranate seeds, lab pearls, basil seeds, and pomegranate juice in a cocktail glass. Garnish with basil leaves and serve with a wide straw so it's easy to suck up the pearls.

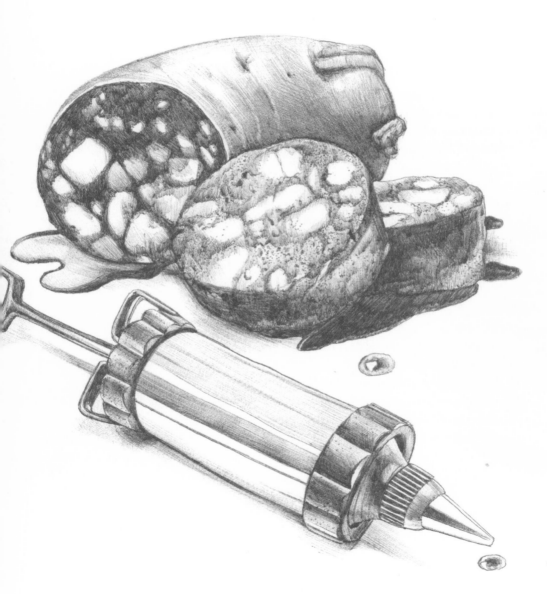

RED MEAT REPLACER

Which meat lover doesn't like the sight of red juices dripping from a freshly grilled steak? While steaks carved from actual, once-living cattle may become a thing of the past, that doesn't mean that diners have to give up the pleasure of red meat. Contrary to popular belief, the appetizing color of red meat isn't due to blood, but to myoglobin, both a protein and a red-hued pigment. Red meat replacer is an all-natural concoction of myoglobin in an appetizing suspension of lab-grown collagen, fat and water. Load the included syringe with red meat replacer and inject your in vitro meat until it's as juicy and plump as you want. There's no need to stop at meat that's naturally red — try some with chicken or fish for a novel taste experiment.

BLACK PUDDING

- 1 liter red meat replacer
- 2 teaspoons salt
- 350 milliliters steel-cut oatmeal
- 500 milliliters fat, diced
- 1 large onion, diced
- 240 milliliters milk
- 1/2 teaspoons black pepper
- 1 teaspoon allspice

1. Preheat the oven to 160° C. Grease two loaf pans. Mix one teaspoon of salt into the red meat replacer.

2. Bring two and a half cups of water to a boil. Add the oats, lower the heat to a simmer, and cook for 15 minutes.

3. In a large bowl, mix together the red meat replacer, onion, fat, milk, pepper, allspice, oatmeal and remaining salt. Divide the mixture between the two loaf pans. Cover with foil and bake for one hour, until firm.

4. To serve, melt a pat of butter in a skillet. Fry thick slices of the pudding until the edges are browned and slightly crispy.

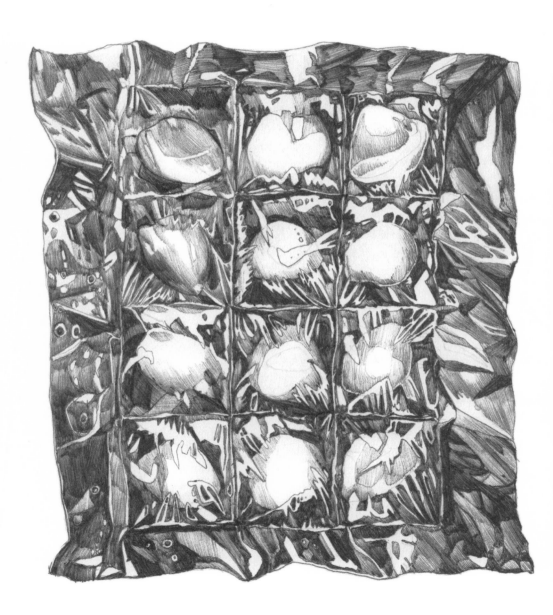

LAB SWEETBREADS

If in vitro meat is not 'exercised' using electricity or mechanical equipment, it develops a melt-in-your-mouth texture that some love and others loathe. True gourmands adore it for its similarity to 'sweetbreads', a culinary term for the pancreas and thymus glands of an animal. While sweetbreads traditionally came from veal calves raised in deplorable conditions and slaughtered at only a few weeks of age, lab sweetbreads are made from wholesome, 100% laboratory-reared muscle cells. These sweetbreads embrace a fresh-from-the-bioreactor aesthetic with minimalistic, single-serving packaging. Unlike animal offal, there's no need to poach them in water or painstakingly remove membranes — lab sweetbreads are edible as-is.

FRIED LAB SWEETBREADS

- 1 kilo lab sweetbreads
- 240 milliliters buttermilk, shaken
- 125 grams flour
- 60 grams cornmeal
- 2 teaspoons paprika
- 1/2 teaspoon cayenne
- 1/2 teaspoon black pepper
- Salt
- Vegetable oil

① Whisk the buttermilk and ½ teaspoon of salt together in a bowl. Add the sweetbreads and soak for one hour in the refrigerator.

② Pur seven centimeters of oil into a pot, work or Dutch oven. Heat the oil to 180° C. Preheat the oven to 200° C.

③ In a shallow dish, whisk together the flour, cornmeal, spices and ½ teaspoon salt. Drain the sweetbreads. Roll each one in the flour mixture, shaking off excess flour.

④ Fry the sweetbreads in batches, cooking each batch for three minutes, until the meat has cooked through and the batter is golden. Drain on a paper towel-lined baking sheet and season to taste with salt. Keep the sweetbreads warm in the oven until ready to serve.

RUSTIC IN VITRO

Many people dismiss lab-grown meat as slick, soulless and completely artificial. Slow-food enthusiasts and organic-only eaters feel uncomfortable dining on a food that seems utterly divorced from centuries of traditional farming and cooking. In response to these concerns, rustic in vitro bioreactors bring artisanal production methods back to cultured meats. The shapes of these bioreactors recall primal cuts of beef or whole Spanish hams. As the meat grows over the course of several months, it develops deep, complex flavors that range from black truffle to oak. The longer rustic in vitro is left to ripen, the more character the replicating cells acquire.

CANTALOUPE
GAZPACHO

- 1 small cantaloupe
- 4 tomatoes
- 2 tablespoons chopped red onion
- Juice of one lemon
- 120 milliliters extra virgin olive oil
- 6 strips of rustic in vitro meat, jamón iberico style
- Salt and pepper

① Scoop the cantaloupe from its peel, and remove all the seeds. Peel the tomatoes and cut them into quarters. Put the cantaloupe, tomatoes, red onion and lemon in a blender and process until extremely smooth.

② With the motor still running, drizzle in the olive oil. Season the soup to taste, and chill in the refrigerator.

③ While the gazpacho is chilling, fry the rustic in vitro in a pan until crispy.

④ When completely chilled, divide the gazpacho into six bowls. Crumble one strip of rustic in vitro into each bowl as a garnish.

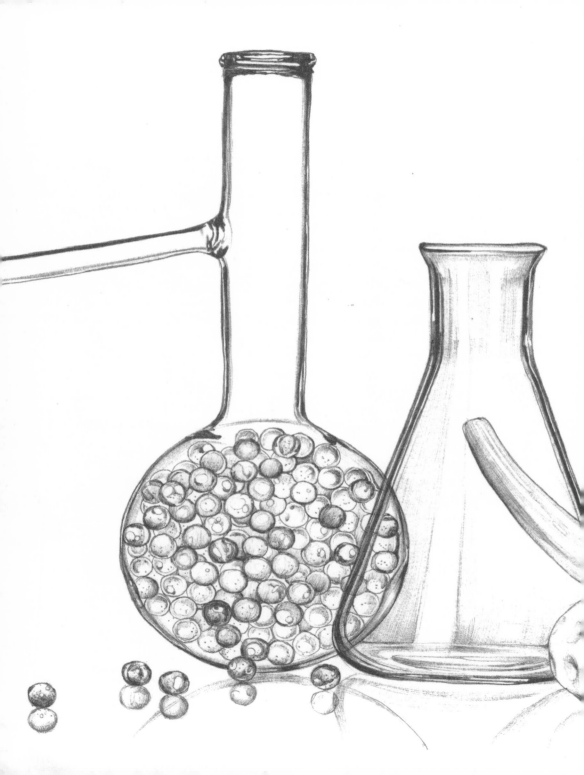

HONEST FROM THE LAB

The need for transparency is a major societal trend in politics, finance and also food. In vitro meat is typically seen as inferior fake meat, but if we move beyond mimicking existing meat products and present it as an honest, healthy, sustainable, safe and transparent product from the lab, in vitro meat could gain an authenticity of its own.

Post, the man behind the world's first lab-grown hamburger, aims for no less than a total transformation of the way we produce meat. "My goal," he says, "is to replace the entirety of livestock production with cultured meat." Post's relaxed manner belies the scale of his ambitions: "I dream that, at some point, McDonald's will approach me to produce all the hamburgers, all over the world." By raising meat entirely in a lab, starting with stem cells and ending with full-grown muscle, Post hopes to make meat that's cheaper, healthier, and more sustainable than the real thing. The everyday quality of the bioreactors in his facility acts as a metaphor for in vitro meat itself: a science-fictional achievement that aspires to not only be normal, but natural.

In Post's office, strewn with balloons from his latest award, we sit down for a discussion about his plans for in vitro meat. Post is confident that we're witnessing the final days of intensive, factory-style farming. "There is no future for traditional meat," he insists, and the end couldn't come sooner. Livestock is responsible for 15% of greenhouse gas emissions worldwide, a number that's poised to keep growing along with the global middle class. Rearing animals for meat is a terrific waste of edible grains, arable land, and clean water, not to mention the fact that emerging diseases often use livestock as a stepping-stone to human populations. It were not these concerns, however, that funded the €250,000 burger, but one very wealthy and very famous animal lover. Sergey Brin, the co-founder of Google and the 'mystery' investor behind Post's in vitro efforts, is strongly motivated by his discomfort with killing animals for food. Post himself seems a bit perplexed, although happily so, by Brin's limitless faith in the project. "He thinks that I can do this on my own in two to five years," Post says, "if he gives me enough money. And, basically, he sees no limit in how much money he can give me." Post himself is more modest about the timeline for commercial implementation. He predicts that within five to six years the cost of in vitro beef will hover around €65 per kilo — less than the most expensive cuts of Wagyu cattle, but still far above what the average shopper can afford.

We're witnessing the final days of intensive factory style farming

Often breathlessly described as 'revolutionary' and 'groundbreaking', in vitro meat is actually a clever repackaging of existing technologies: the cell-culture equivalent of an iPhone. The fact that Post repackages, and doesn't strictly innovate, is at odds with an academic culture that looks down on celebrity, media attention, and researchers who don't conduct 'pure' research. "I don't care about my reputation as a scientist, to be honest," Post says. Given the nature of Sergey Brin's support, this disregard might have to be a requirement. Impatient with the glacial pace of scientific research in universities, Brin has mandated that Post and his team work alone.

Post takes a philosophical angle on this results-minded approach to science: "If we transform ugly pieces of technology into something that is very elegant and useful for the planet and for people, then I'll be perfectly happy."

Our great-grandchildren may shake their heads over our barbaric extraction of 'chicken' from a living animal

If Post's technology becomes commercially viable, it will represent one of the most fundamental changes to the way we approach meat since our ancestors domesticated animals. Our inborn taste for meat drove our evolution and has, in the last few centuries, utterly transformed the face of the earth. Yet Post readily dismisses our 2-million-year-old love affair with meat. In a statement that might be met with skepticism from ranchers and bacon-loving hipsters alike, Post argues that "We don't extract any happiness from eating meat. We don't extract any particular nourishing value from it. It is basically the taste, the color, the texture and the emotions associated with it. Eventually, I think, we will completely dissociate meat from its traditional form." If Post has his way, our great-grandchildren may shake their heads over our barbaric extraction of 'chicken' from a living animal, in the same way we now shudder at the idea of bloodletting or human sacrifice.

However, successfully decoupling meat from its animal origin will only be possible if in vitro meat is identical to the real thing. Post is adamant that lab-grown meat is not only no different from conventional meat, but that it is inherently natural — or, at least, that it is no less natural than anything else we eat. By way of comparison, he emphasizes the gulf between artisanal cheese and the mass-market product we get in grocery stores. Made from the powdered, homogenized milk of hundreds of cows, industrial cheese could not be more different from the small-scale stuff in farmer's markets.

49

Yet supermarket cheese looks like cheese, smells like cheese, and tastes like cheese, Post points out, so we're content to call it cheese. As goes cheese, so goes in vitro meat. "I want it to be exactly the same product as the meat that comes from livestock. Then," he adds, "I would have all the reason to call it 'meat'. How unnatural can that be?"

The lamb-tuna steak will be one of his next projects

Post's own eating habits have informed his attitudes about consumer preference in food and, by extension, in lab-grown meat. He's eaten the same ham-and-cheese sandwich for the last five years — in fact, there's one sitting on his desk as we speak — but he longs for change at dinnertime. "People want boring," he says, "they want something that is reproducible. They want to know what they are buying." But, he continues, our need for predictability is tempered by our love of novelty: new foods, new clothes, new ideas. In vitro meat's first stab at the sweet spot of 'predictable novelty' will be in the realm of processed meat, arguably the worst category of food. Made from the carcass discards of low-quality cows, most of which lived short, miserable lives, there's little redeeming culinary or cultural value in a factory-farmed burger. "Fifty percent of the meat market is already processed meat." Posts says. "We can make a big step forward if we transform just that part of the industry."

Processed meat is the first, but certainly not the only category of meat that in vitro meat will replace. Post is currently working on creating a steak, a far more complex structure that he hopes to build with fat, muscle and a 3D printer. While Post initially dismissed a steak as too ambitious, he's come around to the belief that steak actually makes a stronger argument for the merits of in vitro meat than a hamburger does. While a 'real' burger consists of the ground-up scraps from all parts of an animal, a steak is the purest form of meat. Rather than replacing the leftovers, Post now aims to replicate the main attraction.

The benefits of in vitro meat are so clear that they're in some ways its least interesting aspect. Instead of thinking about what cultured meat doesn't do — pollute, harm animals — it's perhaps more compelling to imagine the new, avant-garde products that it will make possible. Though Post's emphasis on recreating burgers and steaks is decidedly commercial, he's willing to indulge in some more outlandish ideas. "I have these images of hybrids of flamingos and giraffes, a minotaur, or a lamb with a rabbit head," he says, going on to describe the lamb-tuna steak that will be one of his next projects. By mixing stem cells from tuna and sheep, it may be possible to create truly hybrid muscle tissue — a Frankenstein-esque assemblage, no genetic modification necessary. In the realm of the slightly more practical, Post mentions the possibility of "a prescription hamburger that lowers your cholesterol" and even culturing tiger tissue for traditional Chinese medicine — though Post prefers to distance himself from a practice with "no scientific basis".

At the end of our interview, Post opens a drawer and pulls out a hard, dried, hockey puck of an object. This brown lump is the world's second in vitro hamburger, which Post had plasticized for posterity after its grand debut in London. "I was thinking about the possibility of giving it to a museum," he says. "But I'm not sure what kind of museum would exhibit it."

BY KOERT VAN MENSVOORT, ALESSIA ANDREOTTI AND ALLISON GUY

Will pigs, chickens and cows soon be relieved of their millennia-old duty to be our dinner? Fish could swim without the fear of nets and hooks. And humans could finally enjoy a carnivorous lifestyle without any of the guilt. In vitro meat promises that no one will get hurt. While some vegetarians will be overjoyed to be able to eat 'victimless' steak, others won't be so sure that in vitro meat will mean we've solved our dysfunctional relationship with animals. Will we be done with livestock for good? And what will happen to all of the human traditions and industries that depend on rearing — and killing — animals?

POOKIE

SPECIE: SUS DOMESTICUS
GENDER: FEMALE
AGE: 5 YEARS
WEIGHT: 230 KG
COLOUR: PINK
NATURE: JAUNTY

DIET: LEAVES, ACORNS, FRUITS

HARVESTED: 20.01.14
GARDEN: S-W 3A 1278

Pig In The Garden is a reminder that meat traditionally comes from living animals, and the stem cells for in vitro meat still do. Communities that pride themselves on a local, back-to-the-earth approach to food production may raise hogs in shared gardens or yards. Rather than slaughtering their pig, the neighborhood could use it as a living reservoir of stem cells to grow in vitro meat. A trained veterinarian sedates the pig and extracts the cells, which are then used to grow pork in acommunal bioreactor. The pig itself could become a beloved ambassador of the community. Locals will stop by to give their neighborhood pig a scratch or bring it table scraps from home.

BACKYARD PIG ROAST

- 1 pig in the garden roast, approximately 100 kilos
- 2.5 kilos coarse-grain salt
- 75 banana leaves

① Dig a hole large enough to accommodate the roast. Fill the hole completely with a hardwood such as mesquite. Cover the wood with large, flat river rocks. Pour an entire can of lighter fluid through the cracks in the rocks and light a fire. Let the fire burn for two hours.

② Generously salt the roast, inside and outside. Soak several burlap sacks in water.

③ Spread the rocks at the bottom of the pit in an even layer. Cover the rocks with half the banana leaves. Place the roast on top of the banana leaves. Completely cover the roast with the remainder of the banana leaves. Cover the leaves with the wet burlap sacks. Be sure to cover any steam holes. Lay a plastic tarp on top of the pit and seal the tarp with dirt.

④ Let the roast cook for 12 to 16 hours. Dig up the roast and carefully remove it from the banana leaves. Shred the meat with tongs.

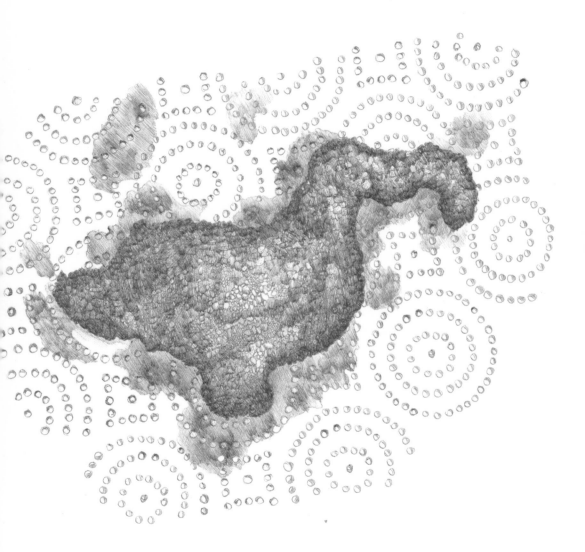

DODO NUGGETS

The dodo has returned! To the dinner table, at least. Thanks to a dried dodo specimen in the Oxford University Museum of Natural History, it becomes possible to sample what the first sailors to visit Mauritius did in 1598. Tissue engineering and advanced genetic sequencing allow food scientists to resurrect the living flesh of this long-extinct species. Kids go crazy for the crispy flavor of cutting-edge science, especially when served with a honey mustard dipping sauce. In this recipe, Dodo Nuggets are used as the 'bread' for a bacon and blue cheese sandwich, perfect for serving as a snack on game day.

DOUBLE DELIGHTS

- 180 milliliters sour cream
- 320 milliliters mayonnaise
- 1 teaspoon Worchestershire sauce
- 1/2 teaspoon dry mustard
- 1/2 teaspoon garlic powder
- 1/2 teaspoon salt
- 1/2 teaspoon freshly ground black pepper
- 120 grams blue cheese, crumbled
- 1 family-size package of dodo nuggets, thawed
- 15 strips of bacon
- Vegetable oil

① Combine the first eight ingredients in a large bowl. Whisk together until well combined. Cover the bowl and store the sauce in the refrigerator.

② Fry the bacon until crispy. Cut each strip in half and drain on a paper-towel lined plate. Reserve the bacon fat in the pan.

③ Working in batches, pan-fry the nuggets in the bacon fat until golden brown and heated through. Add vegetable oil as needed.

④ To assemble the double delights: add a dollop of blue cheese sauce to a nugget, along with a half-strip of bacon. Add another dollop and press a second nugget on top. Repeat this process with the remaining nuggets.

PAINLESS FOIE GRAS

The production of foie gras is a matter of bitter contention between gastronomes and animal rights activists. While the buttery flavor of foie gras is incomparable, there's no disputing that gavage — the force-feeding of geese or ducks using a metal tube — is an inhumane practice. Tissue engineering could solve the perennial controversy of foie gras by growing goose livers without the goose.

By culturing goose liver in a serum rich in growth hormones and nutrients, tissue engineers may be able to perfectly replicate the taste of traditional foie gras. Though French farmers may decry the disembodied livers and the loss of centuries-old practices, this once-rare food could become abundant and affordable — in fact, pump jugs of pate de foie gras may appear alongside ketchup and mayonnaise at fast food joints.

FRIED FOIE GRAS

- 500 grams foie gras, frozen
- 240 milliliters buttermilk
- 250 grams self-rising flour
- 1 tablespoon salt
- 2 teaspoons freshly ground black pepper
- Canola or peanut oil

① Cut the frozen foie gras into long, thin strips. Return the strips back to the freezer.

② Pour the buttermilk in a bowl. In a second bowl, whisk together the flour, salt and pepper. Dredge each fry in the buttermilk, then in the flour mixture.

③ Pour seven centimeters of oil into a pot, wok or Dutch oven. Heat the oil to 180° C. Deep fry the foie gras strips for 10 to 15 seconds, until light golden in color. Drain on paper towels. Serve with ketchup, mayonnaise, or shaved white truffles.

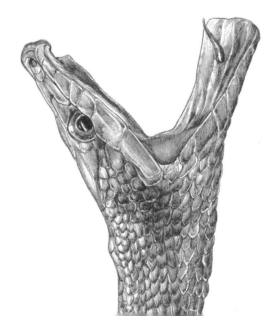

CRUELTY-FREE PET FOOD

Ethical pet owners have long faced a dilemma. Being an animal lover means you often have to feed other animals to your pet, whether it's a rat to your python or canned meat to your cat. With in vitro meat there will be no worries than another animal had to suffer to fill Fido's belly. In vitro pet food is 100% meat and still 100% animal-friendly. Unlike normal pet food, which is made from low-quality scrap meat, Cruelty-Free Pet Food comes from cultured meat raised in sterile conditions without antibiotics, growth hormones or weird chemicals. You'll feel great, and so will your pet.

CRUNCHY KITTY COOKIES

- 1 can of cruelty-free pet food
- 100 grams ground oats
- 1 egg
- 1 tablespoon olive oil
- 1 tablespoon catnip

① Preheat the oven to 180° C. Drain the can of cruelty-free pet food. In a food processor, blend the meat, oat flour, olive oil and catnip until a smooth paste forms.

② Roll the paste into balls and place on a baking sheet lined with parchment paper. Gently press the balls down using a fork.

③ Bake the cookies for 10 minutes, until they are slightly browned around the edges. Store in an airtight container.

★ ☆ ☆ ☆ ☆

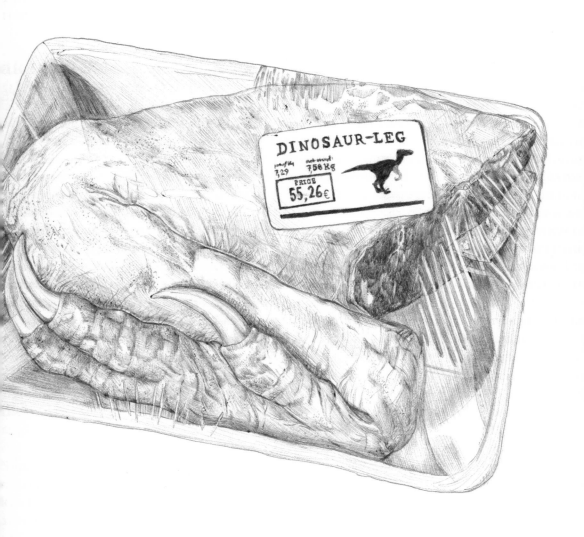

DINOSAUR-LEG

price/kg   net weight:
7,29   7,58 kg

PRICE
55,26€

DINOSAUR LEG

Sorry, Jurassic Park — genetic material only has a half-life of about 500 years, so there's no intact dinosaur DNA left to clone. For diners who still want a taste of Velociraptor au vin, however, here's the next best thing: by coaxing chicken tissue to grow around 3D-printed bones, food scientists could create giant, anatomically-accurate models of dinosaur parts. One Utahraptor leg or Protoceratops thigh is enough to feed the whole (extended) family.

This recipe is a playful take on the old standby of roast chicken and potatoes. Kids get a kick out of the prehistoric-looking 'eggs' — actually colorful potatoes — while everyone loves the crispy skin and bold, Peruvian-inspired spices.

ROAST RAPTOR WITH 'DINOSAUR EGGS'

- 17 kilo dinosaur leg
- 3 tablespoons kosher salt
- 4 kilos small potatoes, a mixture of purple, red and gold varieties
- 250 milliliters vegetable oil
- 250 milliliters vinegar
- 12 cloves garlic
- 4 teaspoons each chile powder, cumin, paprika, soy sauce, chopped fresh oregano and mint

① Rub the dinosaur with the kosher salt. Place in a large resealable plastic bag, press out the air, and chill in the refrigerator for two days.

② Peel and mash the garlic. Mix it with the vegetable oil, vinegar, spices and herbs. Pour the marinade into the bag with the dinosaur. Refrigerate one day.

③ Preheat the oven to 200° C. Toss the potatoes with oil, salt and pepper. Line a roasting pan with the potatoes. Place the dinosaur leg on top.

④ Roast the dinosaur for one hour, stirring the potatoes halfway through. Continue to roast until a meat thermometer reads 70° C when inserted in the thickest part of the leg. Let the dinosaur rest for 15 minutes before carving and serving.

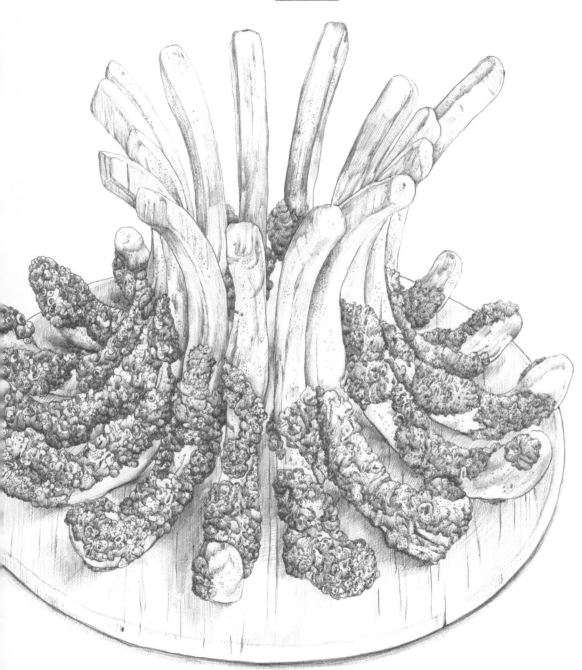

MEAT MOSS

Moss and in vitro meat share one important feature: neither needs veins in order to grow. Meat Moss takes the moss analogy one step further by creating cultured meat with a springy, honeycomb-like texture. The Meat Moss kit replicates a crown roast, concealing a bioreactor within a circle of 'ribs'. The bioreactor extrudes a mossy matrix of meat that gradually covers the ribs and cures in the air. With its porous structure, Meat Moss quickly dries when exposed to air, instead of spoiling. This protein can be peeled off the bone and eaten like beef jerky, or rehydrated in hot broth to take the place of dried tofu, seaweed, or mushrooms.

MEAT MOSS RISOTTO

- 1,200 liters stock
- 50 grams thin asparagus
- 250 grams dried Meat moss
- 50 grams olive oil
- 25 grams butter
- 1 medium onion, minced
- 350 grams Arborio rice
- 1 handful grated Parmesan cheese
- 1 tablespoon parsley, minced
- Salt and pepper

① Rehydrate the Meat Moss in 500 milliliters of boiling water. Set aside for 30 minutes, then drain.

② Trim and discard the tough ends of the asparagus. Chop them into bite-sized pieces, reserving the tips.

③ Melt butter and olive oil in a skillet on medium heat. Sauté the onions until translucent. Add the asparagus and meat, cook for one minute. Add the rice and stir to combine.

④ Add 250 milliliters of stock, stirring constantly, until all of the liquid has been absorbed. Add the stock 250 milliliters at a time, waiting for it to be absorbed in between additions. Cook the rice until it is tender but still al dente, about 20 minutes. Season to taste with salt and pepper. Stir in the parsley, asparagus tips, and half the cheese. Serve sprinkled with the remaining cheese on top.

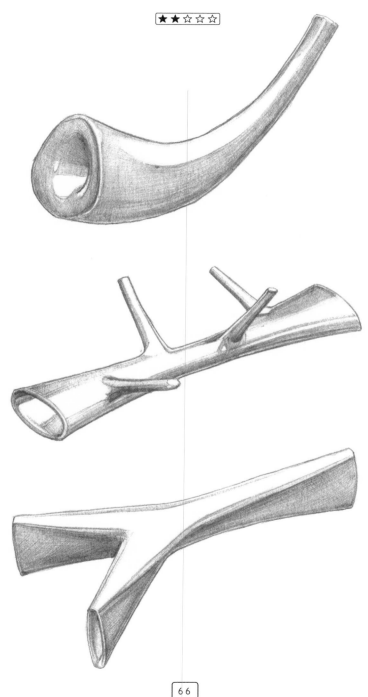

BONE PICKERS

There's something deeply satisfying about eating meat from the bone. Once meat will be disembodied and grown in a lab, diners will be deprived of one of the primal pleasures we share with wolves and lions. Made of cultured meat grown around an ersatz bone scaffold, Bone Pickers satisfy our carnal appetite for gnawing and ripping. The bone doubles as a useful handle, just like a chicken's leg bone or a crown roast of lamb, so diners don't have to get their fingers dirty. After a meal, a pile of beautiful, abstracted bones remains, which can be handed to the family dog or recycled to create the next round of Bone Pickers.

MIDDLE EASTERN BONE SKEWERS

- 600 grams lamb-style bone pickers
- 1 medium onion, cut in quarters 1 garlic clove
- 4 parsley sprigs
- 3 tablespoons lemon juice
- 1 teaspoon lemon zest
- 1/2 teaspoon ground cumin
- 1/2 teaspoon ground coriander
- 1/2 tablespoon salt
- Vegetable oil
- Yoghurt sauce

① Combine the onion, garlic, parsley, lemon juice and zest, cumin, coriander and salt in a blender. Process until it's all smooth.

② Pour the marinade into a resealable plastic bag. Add the bone pickers, turning to coat. Refrigerate for at least six hours, preferably overnight.

③ Light a grill or preheat a grill pan. Remove the bone pickers from the bag, shaking off the excess marinade. Brush each picker with a light coating of vegetable oil. Grill for about five minutes, turning occasionally, until charred around the edges. Serve them drizzled with yoghurt sauce.

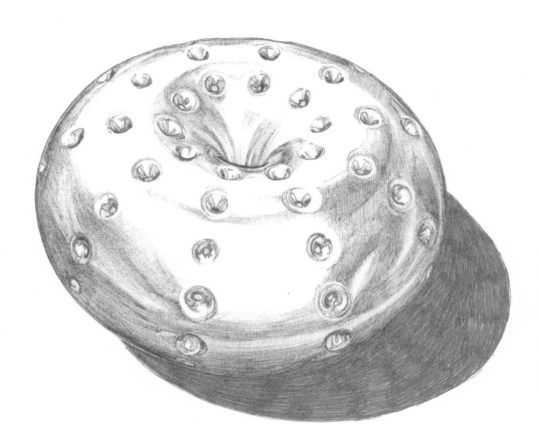

MARROW EGG

Throughout human history, eggs and bone marrow have been one of the most sought-after sources of protein and fat. In fact, the need to smash apart bones to get at the marrow may have been one of the forces that drove our ancestors to adopt stone tools. In a continuation of these ancient tastes, the stylized Marrow Egg takes the buttery goodness of marrow and packages it with the convenience of an egg.

These dainty 'eggs' aren't filled with yolk, however, but with snow-white cultured marrow. The 3D-printed exterior is inspired by the 'test', or shell, of a sea urchin, and adds valuable calcium to a dish. Lab-grown Marrow Eggs lend meaty notes to vegetarian soups, and taste delicious when roasted and spread on toast — no stone club required.

ROASTED MARROW EGGS

- 8 marrow eggs
- 1/2 bunch parsley
- 2 shallots, thinly sliced
- 2 tablespoons olive oil
- 1 tablespoon lemon juice
- 1 tablespoon capers
- Black pepper
- Salt
- 8 slices of thick, rustic-style bread

① Preheat the oven to 230° C. In a small bowl, toss the parsley with the shallots, olive oil, lemon juice and capers. Season to taste.

② Place the breadslices on a baking sheet and toast until golden brown. Remove the bread from the oven.

③ Place the marrow eggs on a rimmed baking sheet with the open sides pointing up. Roast for 15 minutes, until the marrow begins to melt.

④ Divide the marrow and parsley salad between four plates. Serve with the toast and a long, thin spoon to scoop out the marrow.

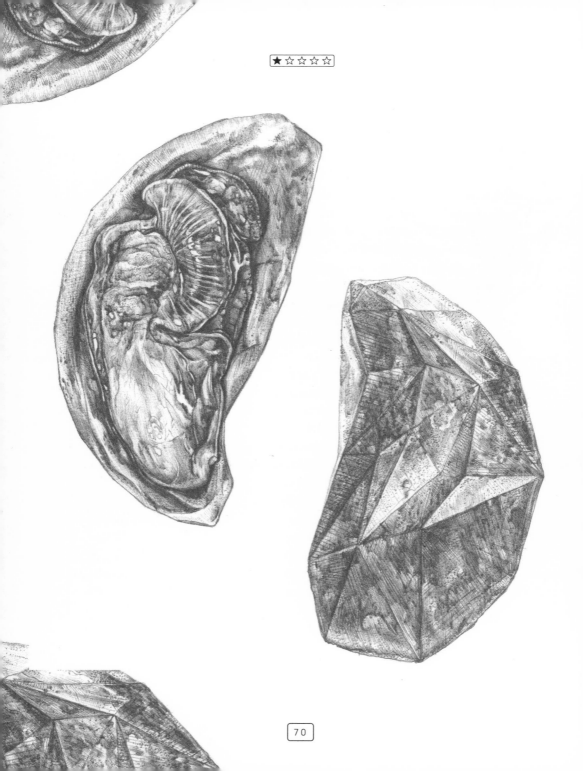

IN VITRO OYSTERS

Bathed in a warm sea of serum, row upon row of miniature bioreactors nurture small morsels of flesh. Twice a day the nutrient rich tide recedes, triggering the muscles to contract and clamp the hinged halves of their bioreactors tightly shut. It's this cycle that gives the In Vitro Oysters their much-lauded texture.

When the muscle has fully grown, the oysters are pried from their electrical connections and shipped to lab-food markets and high-end restaurants. Connoisseurs may become adept at picking out the terroir of each lab, from the briny metal overtones of Atlantic serum to the sweeter, more rounded flavor from Pacific facilities. As ocean-based oyster beds have all but vanished, In Vitro Oysters may prove an exquisite alternative.

VIANDE-HUÎTRES GRILLÉES

- 12 unopened in vitro oysters
- 1 shallot, minced
- 120 milliliters white wine
- 115 grams unsalted butter, divided in 8 pieces
- 1 teaspoon each chopped chervil, chives and parsley

① Preheat a grill. Simmer the shallot and wine in a small saucepan over medium heat until the wine has reduced by half.

② Remove the saucepan from the heat. Add the butter piece by piece, whisking to combine. Stir in the herbs.

③ Grill the oysters until the bioreactor just opens, three to five minutes. Carefully pry away the top half of the bioreactor, taking care not to spill any of the serum inside. Cut the muscle to separate it from the bioreactor's lower half. Arrange the oysters on a platter. Spoon a portion of the sauce over each oyster and serve immediately.

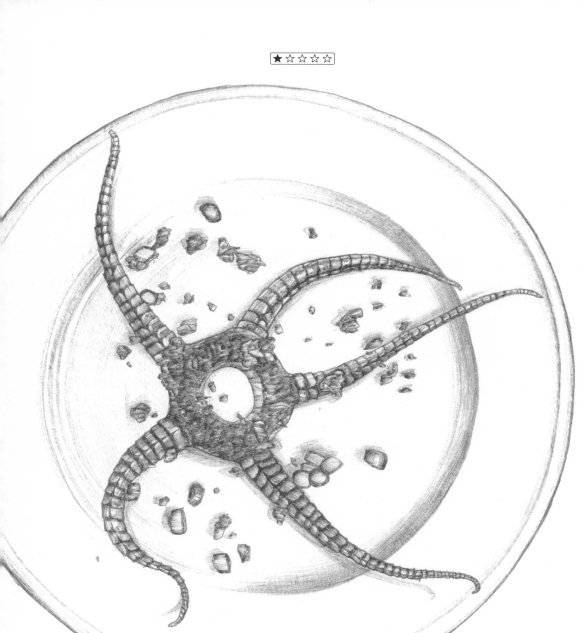

THE THROAT TICKLER

Wet, slippery, and wriggling, this curious 'creature' lives on the border between a sea anemone and a sex toy. The Throat Tickler beckons from your plate with come-hither motions, and slides its tentacles around your lips as you slurp it down.

Because Throat Ticklers have no organs or nervous systems, they're not truly alive. Rather, their enticing movement is caused by sodium altering the voltage differentials across cell membranes, triggering the muscle tissue to contract. A pinch of salt will incite a sensual wave of the Throat Tickler's tentacles, as will any salty sauce. Never before has a tickle in your throat been such a hedonistic experience.

DANCING ANEMONE RICE BOWL

- 1 throat tickler
- 1 tablespoon grated wasabi
- 2 tablespoons salmon roe
- Seasoned sushi rice or cooked rice noodles
- 1 teaspoon chopped mitsuba (wild Japanese parsley)
- Soy sauce

① Add a scoop of rice to a bowl. Top the rice with the wasabi and fish roe, and sprinkle with the mitsuba.

② Add the throat tickler to the rice bowl. Pour the soy sauce over the tickler. Consume while the tickler is still moving. Note: serve the tickler immediately after removing it from its bioreactor. Muscle cells will die if left out too long, and the throat tickler will not react to the soy sauce.

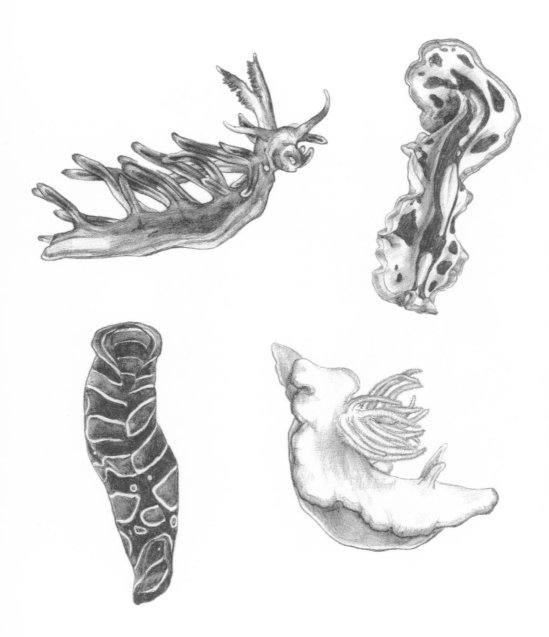

A must-have for corner offices and seafood restaurants, the In Vitro Aquarium combines the soothing qualities of a fish tank with easy access to sushi-grade meat. A glass-paneled bioreactor filled with a growth serum provides the habitat for dozens of strikingly colored in vitro 'species'. Electrical pulses force the cultured muscle tissue to contract, causing these semi-living creatures to swim gracefully through the tank.

These 'species' aren't just lovely in a liquid medium, but make animated additions to teppanyaki grills outfitted with an electrical current. The lab-grown creatures skitter and slither across the electrified surface, cooking as they scoot along. Competitive diners may place bets on whose food will be the fastest.

SPEAR FISHING FOR THE SEMI-LIVING

- 500 grams in vitro animals, any species
- 6 tablespoons honey
- 3 tablespoons soy sauce
- 3 tablespoons rice vinegar
- 1/2 pineapple cut into bite-sized cubes
- Wooden skewers
- Vegetable oil

① Preheat an electrified flat griddle. Lightly brush the griddle with vegetable oil.

② Whisk together the honey, soy sauce and rice vinegar. Divide the sauce between four bowls, give a bowl and collection of skewers to each diner.

③ Grill the pineapple cubes until lightly charred on all sides.

④ Place the in vitro animals on the griddle, and turn on the electric current. Encourage diners to spear the animals as they move across the griddle. The pineapple and meat is best when dipped in the sauce.

PIG IN THE BACKYARD

Since animals need not be slaughtered
in the production of in vitro meat,
the technology may give rise to new
human-animal relations. Pigs in urban
backyards could serve as the living
donors for muscle stem cells through
biopsies every now and then. While
the pigs live happy lives as companion
animals, feeding on our waste food, their
cells are cultured in local meat factories.

ESSAY BY COR VAN DER WEELE AND CLEMENS DRIESSEN

Perhaps the most uplifting promise of in vitro meat is that it will be good for animals. Animal cells are needed to make it, but only in small amounts, and if algae can be used to feed these cells, no animals need to suffer for this meat. In 2008, the animal rights organization PETA (People for the Ethical Treatment of Animals) offered one million dollars to whoever could develop marketable in vitro chicken by 2012[1]. As that deadline proved to be too tight, PETA used the money to subsidize in vitro meat research. Many other people, too, welcome in vitro meat primarily because of what it may mean for animals. Even though they often find the idea strange and perhaps even a bit uncanny, the promise for animals is widely felt as a source of hope.

The background of this hope is not hard to understand. While the global consumption of meat is rising steadily, its moral reputation is shrinking, at least in Western societies. The problems associated with meat are becoming ever more widely known and discussed: animal suffering in factory farming, alarming greenhouse gas emissions, enormous and ever expanding use of land, water and energy. Moreover, all these problems are deepening as the growing world population is expected to double its meat consumption in the coming decades.

Most people know or surmise something about these problems, and they feel uneasy about them, especially about the fate of animals in factory farming. More than ten years ago, a Danish study already found that meat eaters were almost as negative about meat as non-meat eaters, especially because of intensive animal farming[2]. Yet most of us continue to love and eat meat. How is this possible? Are we really indifferent, deep down? That is what Jonathan Safran Foer thinks: "We can't plead ignorance, only indifference."[3]

While the global consumption of meat is rising steadily, its moral reputation is shrinking

But there is reason to doubt this. Unease is a sign of ambivalence, which is not the same as indifference: it does not signal the absence of concern, but tension, in this case between fondness of meat and concern for animals. The difference may be hard to tell in practice, because ambivalence does not necessarily result in action. One of the ways to deal with the psychological discomfort of ambivalence is turning away from unwelcome information. Such 'strategic ignorance' is typically not completely conscious, and it is a paradoxical phenomenon: turning away from learning more because you're not indifferent[4,5]. There are many signs that strategic ignorance is a frequent and routine way of dealing with ambivalence about meat. "If you want to eat meat, you should not know too much about it", is an example of what people say, or "If I paid attention to every factory farmed chicken, shopping would be much more expensive."[6] Judging from their behavior, such people may look indifferent, while in fact they cope with ambivalence through strategic ignorance. This coping strategy is aided by the invisibility of factory farming and the invisibility of the animal origin of many meat products. But as the shadowy aspects of meat are becoming more widely discussed, it becomes ever more difficult not to be troubled by meat.

The alleged unnaturalness of in vitro meat may be precisely what we are looking for

In vitro meat takes both the love for meat and the unease about it seriously. In the first moral review of in vitro meat, Hopkins and Dacey[7] framed in vitro meat precisely as a way for meat eaters to eat meat with a clear conscience. This is also what we find in responses towards the idea of in vitro meat in interviews and workshops. The idea of moral hope dominates, for animals as well as for our conscience. Even people whose first response is to recoil from the idea ("yuck!") tend to quickly realize the promise: "But wait a minute; when I think of what it might mean for animals, it already looks different."[8] That in vitro meat is welcomed because it promises a solution for ambivalence about meat and animals was also clear from media responses to Mark Post's proof-of-concept hamburger. As a Daily Telegraph commentator wrote, "This should be a source of unalloyed joy for those of us, like me, who love a good chunk of meat but feel a nagging disquiet knowing that a conscious being had to be bred and then killed in order for me to eat it."[9]

Yet the idea of in vitro meat comes with ambivalences of its own. The idea makes many people hesitant about our food becoming ever more technological, unnatural and industrial. Will it alienate us further from nature and from animals? Wouldn't it be better if we changed our behavior? Does dependence on a technological solution amount to moral laziness? If we care about the quality of our future food systems, we must take these questions seriously — and a further reason to do so is that in vitro meat can only be helpful for animals if it is attractive (enough) for humans. In their discussion of the pros and cons of in vitro meat, Hopkins and Dacey already gave some consideration to these issues. Building partly on their work, and on some of the designs that are shown in this book, we have been holding workshops to explore future scenarios of in vitro meat and why and how they are attractive or unattractive. On the basis of these and other sources, what can we say about the ambivalences of in vitro meat? We will look at two kinds of uneasiness: first about unnaturalness and our relations with nature, then about the idea that in vitro meat promotes moral laziness.

The idea of in vitro meat and its public reception can be considered as a form of inquiry into the meanings of meat

Hopkins and Dacey say that "the alleged unnaturalness" of in vitro meat may be precisely what we are looking for, since at least some of the 'natural' ways of producing meat are very problematic[7]. The latter is certainly true for factory farming. In our workshops we found that every time the unnaturalness of in vitro meat turned up, it was followed by remarks to the effect that factory farming and current meat processing are not very natural either. More generally, discussions on in vitro meat always tended to become discussions on the drawbacks of 'normal' meat.

That does not yet mean that in vitro meat is automatically an inspiring alternative. Simon Fairlie, writing about the future of meat, thinks that in vitro meat will further estrange us from nature and from animals. While the organic sector is campaigning for slow food and real meat, he says, in vitro meat represents the opposite tendency, towards factory-produced forms of protein[10].

While in vitro meat may slowly become less strange, meat as we know it starts to look stranger

In response, it can be argued that even when in vitro meat is produced in big factories, it will be good for our relations with animals, because if in vitro meat replaces factory farming, the lives of the remaining food animals no longer need to be dominated by the all-encompassing need for efficiency. But big factories are not the only option. From one of our workshops a scenario emerged that we called 'the pig in the backyard'. According to this vision of in vitro meat production, pigs in urban backyards serve as the living donors for muscle stem cells through biopsies every now and then. While the pigs live happy lives as companion animals, feeding on our waste food, their cells are cultured in local meat factories. This scenario focuses not on the products of in vitro meat, but on what the technology could mean for human-animal relations through local production.

Workshop participants experienced this scenario as almost too good to be true. Here we have it all, they said: meat, a clear conscience, local production and close contact between humans and animals, which was felt to represent the opposite of alienation from animals[8]. Interestingly, worries about in vitro meat being too technological or unnatural were also absent here. The enthusiasm is an indication that mode and site of production make a difference for the appreciation of in vitro meat, just as they do for 'normal' meat, and that in developing in vitro meat, production processes need as much attention as products.

In vitro meat encourages new perspectives on meat

In later workshops, responses to this scenario were less euphoric. People saw it as really too good to be true, even as utterly unrealistic. After all, it goes against many trends in food production, such as increasing scale, strict standards of hygiene, and the expulsion of food animals from the city. Urban farms were seen as somewhat more realistic than backyards, but even then, a pig-in-the-city scenario can hardly be expected to be the default scenario for in vitro meat. Hamburgers or 'magic meat balls' from factories were seen as much more feasible[11].

At the same time, the prospect of pigs on urban farms touches on other current initiatives. For example, 'Varkenshuis' (Pig House) was an art project that involved the rearing of pigs in public yards as a neighborhood responsibility[12]. It was performed in one village and two cities in the Netherlands. After six to ten months, the pigs were slaughtered and their meat was distributed among the people of the neighborhood. The aim of the project was to bring people in close contact with the animals they eat, to expose and reverse alienation from the sources of our meat. In the cities, emotions in response to the pigs ran high; for example, petitions were organized in both of them to prevent the pigs from being slaughtered. This once again demonstrates that when they know and see, people are anything but indifferent to the fate of animals.

Pig houses partly point in different directions than the scenario of pigs in backyards for in vitro meat. While both aim at closer interaction between humans and animals, one promotes realism about meat that comes from animals, while the other aims at moral purity through technology. Yet it is fascinating to see how old peasant-like traditions and new technology can converge and interact to make us rethink meat, our relations with animals and our moral identities with regard to meat.

In vitro meat thus seems to encourage new perspectives on meat and to inspire moral change long before it is on the market — as this book also exemplifies. But the opposite has been argued as well. In vitro meat may stand in the way of moral change, at least in the short term, precisely because of its technological promise. As a Dutch columnist wrote, in vitro meat does not challenge the addiction to meat but legitimates it. Meat eaters may just keep on "stuffing themselves full of meat", knowing that a technological fix to the problems is in the making[13]. In other words, technology makes for moral laziness.

There is something to the idea that in the short term, in vitro meat may not be much more than a source of hope for many people. Does it therefore stand in the way of moral change? As we see it, this expectation is based on a too narrow view of moral change and its relation to technology. Technology and morality are not necessarily opposing ways of dealing with problems: they can be intertwined.

To begin with, the moral laziness argument seems to assume that moral change necessarily comes down to changes in our values and behavior. Hopkins and Dacey responded to this objection by saying that there are other moral goals than our own virtuousness. Maybe in vitro meat does not help clean our souls, but reducing animal suffering and preventing global environmental destruction are worthwhile moral goals in and of themselves[7]. Technology, in other words, can be developed for moral reasons and for moral goals, and in vitro meat is a clear example. Those who reject in vitro meat as a source of moral change may be too optimistic about behavior change; despite the urgency of a decrease in meat consumption, the global trend is very different.

Imagination is crucial when it comes to redirections of desire and morality

In the long run, a technology, or even the mere idea of a particular technology such as in vitro meat, can also influence moral values[14]. The proposal of in vitro meat may not immediately change meat consumption, yet it further activates existing ambivalences about meat. Slowly but surely it may help to change the moral landscape in which our thoughts and decisions about meat, or protein consumption, take place; the idea of in vitro meat and its public reception can be considered as a form of inquiry into the meanings of meat. These meanings differ among (sub)cultures. It may not be an accident that this inquiry has been initiated in the Netherlands, a country in which kroketten (croquettes), frikandellen, hamburgers and amorphous chicken filets are dominant elements of the food culture. During our workshops, only older people asked whether it would be possible to create particular cuts of meat, for example rib eye or entrecote. Younger generations tended to be happy with hamburgers. Yet regardless of such differences, while in vitro meat may slowly become less strange, meat as we know it starts to look stranger. As The Times editorial said in response to the in vitro meat hamburger presented in August 2013: "How absurd is it to imagine all our meat one day being produced by a tissue culturing process? Not much more absurd than it is to imagine our meat continuing to be produced as it is now."[15]

Such processes of change take place in interaction with other developments, as the pig in the backyard scenario illustrates. In the ongoing questioning of meat, old traditions and new technology may join hands. These new combinations are typically explored in the boundary area of science, art and design, with the imagination as a prominent ingredient.

The American philosopher John Deweyhas argued that the imagination is crucial when it comes to large redirections of desire and morality[16]. If he is right, as we think he is, the need for the imagination in the context of meat and our relations with animals is large. It is a domain where depressing realities exist that make huge amounts of animals unhappy, and many people too, but that have proven to be very hard to change. Peter Singer, the author of Animal Liberation, the book that played such a crucial role in the development of animal ethics[17], has put much hope on in vitro meat[18]. Might in vitro meat indeed become the vehicle of animal liberation that will make us look back in 50 years, wondering how people were ever able to morally tolerate factory farming? For now, much is still open about the moral dynamics generated by in vitro meat. And though there are no recipes for moral change, a cookbook may be a good way to get a taste of the future of meat.

REFERENCES

1. PETA (2012): In vitro meat prize deadline extended. http://www.peta.org/blog/vitro-meat-prize-deadline-extended/(Accessed December 22, 2013).

2. Holm, L. en M. Møhl (2000). The role of meat eating in everyday food culture: an analysis of an interview study in Copenhagen. Appetite 34: 277-283.

3. Foer, J.S. (2009): Eating animals. Little, Brown & Co, New York.

4. Williams, N. (2008). Affected ignorance and animal suffering: why our failure to debate factory farming puts us at moral risk. Journal of Agricultural and Environmental ethics 21: 371-384.

5. Van der Weele, J. (2013). Inconvenient truths: determinants of strategic ignorance in moral dilemmas SSRN, http://papers.ssrn.com/sol3/papers.cfm?abstract_id=2247288(Accessed December 22, 2013)

6. Van der Weele, C. (2013). Meat and the benefits of ambivalence. In: Helena Röcklinsberg and Per Sandin (eds): The ethics of consumption; the citizen, the market and the law. Wageningen Academic Publishers, Wageningen.

7. Hopkins, P. and A. Dacey (2008). Vegetarian meat: could technology save animals and satisfy meat eaters? Journal of Agricultural and Environmental Ethics 21: 579-596.

8. Van der Weele, C. and C. Driessen (2013) Emerging profiles for in vitro meat; ethics through and as design. Animals 3; 647-662

9. Chivers T. (2013) Why I've a healthy appetite for stem-cell meat. The Daily Telegraph, August 6, 17

10. Fairlie, S. (2010). Meat: a benign extravagance. Chelsea green publishing, White River Junction.

11. Van der Weele, C. and C. Driessen (in preparation): Exploring future scenarios for in vitro meat

12. Varkenshuis is een plek voor varkens en mensen. http://varkenshuis.nl/ (In Dutch; accessed December 22, 2013)

13. Van Hintum, M. (2013). Meat addicts can order their daily portion of animal suffering anywhere. Volkskrant, August 7 (in Dutch).

14. Driessen, C. and M. Korthals (2012). Pig Towers and In vitroMeat: Disclosing Moral Worlds by Design. Social Studies of Science 42, 797–820.

15. Leading editorial article (2013) Meat the future, The Times August 6, 24

16. Dewey, J. (1980 / 1934). Art as experience. New York, Perigree.

17. Singer, P. (2009 / 1975) Animal liberation. Harper Perennial modern Classics.

18. Singer, P. (2013). The world's first cruelty-free hamburger. The Guardian, August 5.

The world's population is growing, and growing more affluent. More people than ever before can now afford meat. The demand for animal products is staggering. On the other side of the wealth spectrum, huge portions of humanity cannot afford even basic necessities. For them, access to protein is not a matter of luxury, but of survival. By growing meat entirely in the lab, starting with stem cells and ending with full-grown muscle, it could be possible to produce cheaper, healthier, and more sustainable meat than the original thing. Even if it won't replace gourmet meat like grass-fed beef or heritage chicken breeds, in vitro meat could satisfy the globe's hunger for cheap, abundant animal protein.

DISASTER BARS

Although primarily developed for emergency famine relief, Disaster Bars may become a favorite of campers, cultists, and anyone with an eye out for the end of the world. The ideal food for survival situations, these bars start with a base of dehydrated cultured meat power and rendered in vitro fat and are then enhanced with fiber, vitamins and minerals.

Inspired by pemmican, a Native American food used on long journeys, Disaster Bars are nutritionally complete and shelf-stable for years. While a person can comfortably live on this ready-to-eat meal, fans have come up with creative recipes for when they want a little more variety in their Armageddon meals. This rich birthday cake uses disaster bars and dry ingredients you're likely to have in your hiking backpack or bomb shelter.

APOCALYPTIC BIRTHDAY CAKE

- 220 grams flour
- 90 grams cocoa powder
- 1 teaspoon baking powder
- 2 teaspoon baking soda
- 1 teaspoon salt
- 450 grams sugar
- 240 milliliters milk, reconstituted from powder
- 1 tablespoon hard liquor
- 2 disaster bars
- 40 milliliters boiling water

① Preheat a solar oven or cooking pit to 180° C. Melt the disaster bars in a small saucepan. Remove the protein particles using a coffee filter or scrap of tightly woven cloth. Measure out 120 milliliters of fat.

② In a large bowl, whisk together the dry ingredients. Whisk in the milk, liquor and melted fat, mixing until well combined. Add the boiling water and stir to combine.

③ Pour the batter into a greased round pan. Bake 25 to 30 minutes, until the top is firm and a knife inserted into the middle comes out clean. Cool completely before serving.

★★★★☆

MEDICINAL MEAT BEANS AND RICE

Familiar to billions of people around the world, 'rice and beans' has become a staple dish essentially anywhere where rice and legumes can be grown. Meat Beans And Rice improves on this age-old pairing by adding an animal protein to the mix. The beans are actually small pellets of dried lab-grown meat, which can be supplemented with certain vitamins or medicines that are able to withstand the high heat of cooking. The shape of the beans varies by region and local food traditions. In Central America, for instance, the pellets could be approximate the size of black or pinto beans, while in India, they could be shaped like lentils.

MEDICINAL CONGEE

- 250 gram mix of rice and meat beans
- 1.5 liters vegetable stock
- 1 small knob of ginger, sliced
- 1 teaspoon salt
- 4 shallots, sliced into thin rings
- 6 tablespoons vegetable oil
- 1 bunch of scallions, sliced

① Add the rice, broth, ginger and salt to a pot and bring to a simmer. Reduce the heat to a bare simmer and stir occasionally, until the rice has nearly disintegrated into creamy consistency, about one hour. Add water as needed to adjust the thickness.

② While the rice is cooking, heat the oil in a skillet until shimmering. Fry the shallots until they are golden and crispy, stirring frequently. Remove the shallots to a plate and reserve the oil.

③ When the congee has cooked fully, season to taste with white pepper and additional salt. Serve topped with the crispy shallots, sliced scallions, and a drizzle of shallot oil.

One of the first cultured meat products to hit the market, Meat Powder is the most straightforward form of in vitro meat. Consisting of pure dried protein, meat powder is fat-free and shelf-stable. Nearly flavorless on its own, Meat Powder comes in a rainbow of flavors suitable for a variety of applications, from soups and stews to shakes and baked goods. It could find particular favor in poorer regions where refrigeration and conventional animal protein are expensive or hard to come by. Although envisioned as a cheap staple food, Meat Powder can also be added to gourmet dishes. In this recipe, it forms the basis for a creamy meat fondue. Gather the whole family around a bubbling pot of in vitro gravy for a fun, cozy evening of cooking and chatting.

MEAT POWDER FONDUE

- 100 grams butter
- 200 grams meat powder, beef flavor
- 2 shallots, minced
- 500 milliliters milk
- 500 milliliters beef stock
- 1 tablespoon Dijon mustard
- Salt and pepper

① Melt the butter in a medium saucepan on low heat. Sauté the shallot in the butter until the shallot is softened and translucent.

② When the butter begins to froth, add the meat powder. Whisk until a roux forms and turns a deep golden brown.

③ Add the milk and beef stock and simmer for half an hour, or until the mixture reaches a fondue-like consistency. Stir salt, pepper and Dijon mustard into the mixture. Serve with bread cubes, cheese, or chunks of in vitro meat.

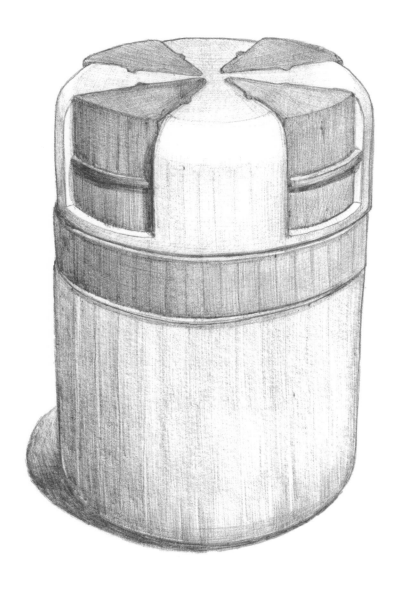

Cup It beefs up instant soup by making it meatier, healthier, and easier than ever. Pop a Cup It capsule in the patented dispenser and enjoy a bowl of hot soup in a matter of seconds. Each capsule is filled with a hearty mixture of dried lab-grown meat and fat, and flavored with all-natural spices, herbs and thickeners.

The self-heating version of the all-in-one cup of soup will be even more convenient. With the click of a button, the soup can heat to over 60° C in only three minutes. It's an ideal food to bring along for camping trips or long commutes. The durable Cup It is expected to find widespread use in military and humanitarian applications where cooking equipment is difficult to come by.

ALMOST INSTANT CHICKEN NOODLE SOUP

- 4 packets Cup It, chicken flavor
- 250 grams instant ramen noodles
- 1 medium onion, chopped
- 2 medium carrots, chopped
- 3 cloves garlic, minced
- 2 ribs celery, chopped
- 1 liter water
- 1 handful parsley, finely chopped
- 2 tablespoons vegetable oil

① Heat the vegetable oil in a large pot until shimmering. Add the onion, garlic, carrots, and celery. Sauté for five minutes, until the vegetables have softened and the onion is translucent.

② Add the water and packets of Cup It to the pot. Bring the liquid to a boil, stirring to dissolve the Cup It powder.

③ Add the instant ramen noodles. Lower the heat and simmer for three minutes, until the noodles have cooked through. Divide the soup between four bowls and serve with parsley.

★★★★☆

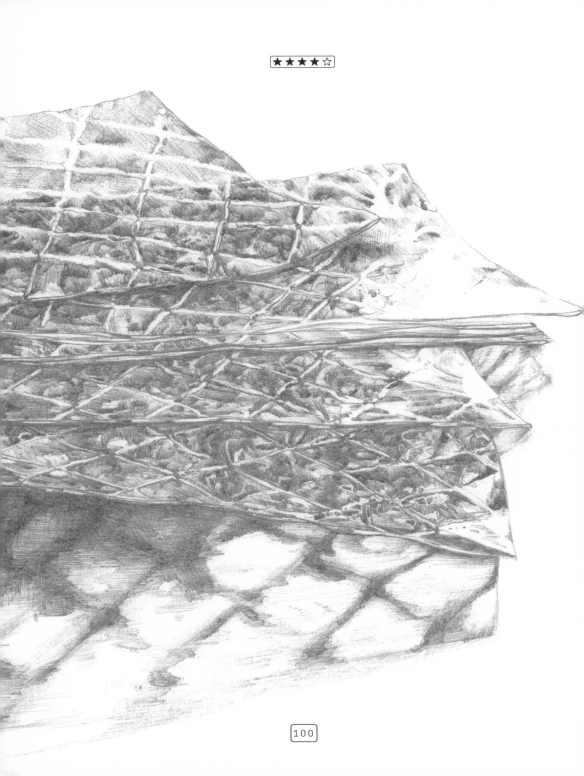

VEGAN GELATIN

Vegetarians and vegans have a hard time avoiding gelatin. This substance, derived from the collagen in animal skin, tendons, ligaments and bones, has made its way into hundreds of products: jelly candy, shampoo, ice cream, paper, cosmetics, capsule coatings for pills, and even the emulsion for black-and-white photos.

Scientists have struggled to come up with a plant-based replacement that manages to match gelatin's unique properties and enormous variety of special applications. Vegan Gelatin is the perfect substitute for conventional gelatin, because it's still actually made from animal tissue. With Vegan Gelatin, fibrous tissues such as tendons or skin could be grown in a lab and then processed to make a cruelty-free replacement for a once ubiquitous animal product.

RAINBOW JELLY

- 3 to 6 boxes flavored gelatin, in different colors
- 1 liter milk
- 4 envelopes unflavored gelatin
- 680 grams vanilla yogurt
- 200 grams sugar
- 1 tablespoon vanilla extract
- Whipped cream
- Rainbow sprinkles

① Pour each color of the flavored gelatin into a separate bowl. To each bowl, add 240 milliliters of boiling water and 120 milliliters of cold water. Mix well.

② Add the milk to a saucepan and heat until lukewarm. Meanwhile, mix the four envelops of gelatin in a large bowl with 240 milliliters of boiling water, stirring to dissolve the gelatin. Whisk the milk, yogurt, sugar and vanilla extract into the bowl.

③ Pour the first color of gelatin into a 33 x 23 centimeter baking pan. Refrigerate until the gelatin has set completely, about 45 minutes. Pour 350 milliliters of the milk mixture on top of the first color, and refrigerate until set. Repeat with the remaining gelatin, alternating the colored and white layers. When finished, refrigerate another hour. To serve, cut the gelatin into slices and top with whipped cream and sprinkles.

SCRAP JERKY

Not all in vitro meat is grade-A certifiable. Some cell cultures can get contaminated with other species — an all-beef culture might wind up with some chicken parts, for instance — or they can develop small, harmless tumors. Other times, a piece of in vitro meat may not be perfectly shaped or colored, likely leading to consumers passing it over in favor of more aesthetically appealing cuts of meat. These otherwise unsellable 'factory seconds' gain a new lease on life by getting ground into a pulp for Scrap Jerky. This meat pulp, like paper pulp, is spread on screens and dried in order to preserve it. An extremely low-cost convenience food, Scrap Jerky could be enlivened by flavorings such as chili pepper, brown sugar or teriyaki. Scrap Jerky may be sold in gas stations and grocery stores.

BRAZILIAN FEIJOADA

- 2 tablespoons vegetable oil
- 1 onion, diced
- 2 cloves of garlic, minced
- 350 grams peelable sausage, sliced in rounds
- 150 grams scrap jerky
- 600 milliliters beef broth
- 1 bay leaf
- Two 400-gram cans black beans, with liquid
- 500 grams cooked white rice, warmed

① Heat the oil in a skillet until shimmering. Add the onion and garlic and cook until the onion is soft and translucent. Add the sausage, scrap jerky, bay leaf and 570 milliliters of the broth. Bring to a boil and cook for 10 minutes, stirring frequently. Add the beans and simmer for 15 minutes. Discard the bay leaf.

② Stir 30 milliliters of the beef broth into the rice.

③ Serve the stew with the rice on the side and either fried plantains or sautéed collard greens.

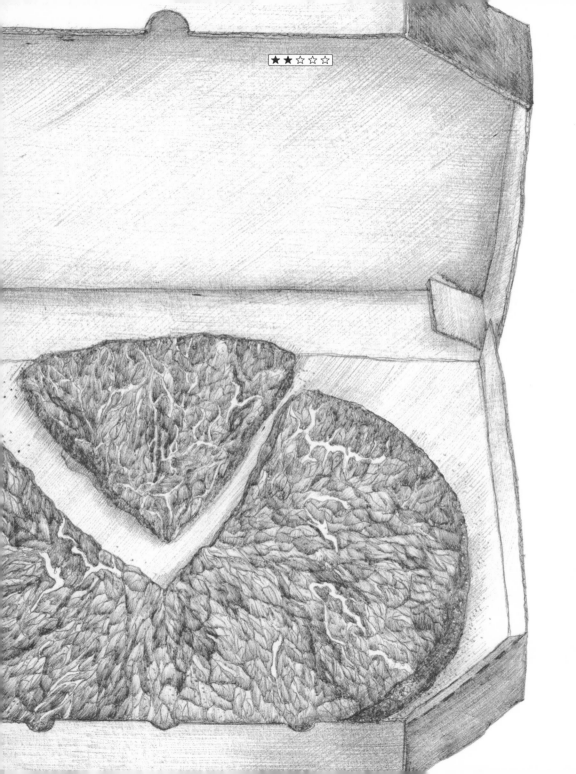

Grown stacked in tall, tube-shaped bioreactors, the Giant Steak makes an affordable steak dinner possible for the entire family. Its circular shape means that there's no more bickering over who gets the rare piece and who gets the well-done one: a single steak is big enough to accommodate all tastes and degrees of doneness.

Local bisteccheria deliver a gourmet meal within half an hour or less, along with standard steak dinner sides like baked potatoes and green beans. This recipe is inspired by the Philadelphia cheesesteak, a famous regional sandwich that incorporates melted cheese and thinly sliced beef.

GIANT CHEESE STEAK

- 1 giant steak
- 1 can of whole peeled tomatoes
- 2 tablespoons olive oil
- 2 cloves garlic
- 1 teaspoon dried oregano
- 1/2 teaspoon red pepper flakes
- 1 teaspoon sugar
- 1 teaspoon salt
- 4 balls of mozzarella, shredded
- Pizza sauce

① Puree in the tomatoes using a blender or food mill. Heat the olive oil in a saucepan. Add the garlic, spices, sugar and salt and cook for three minutes. Add the tomatoes, reduce the heat to the lowest setting, and cook for one hour, stirring occasionally.

② Preheat the broiler or grill function to its highest setting. Lightly oil a baking sheet and pre-warm it in the oven for five minutes.

③ Place the steak on the sheet and broil for four minutes. Remove the steak from the oven, flip it over and top with the tomato sauce, followed by the shredded cheese.

④ Return the steak to the oven and bake for another four minutes, until the cheese has melted and is lightly browned around the edges. Cut the steak into slices and serve.

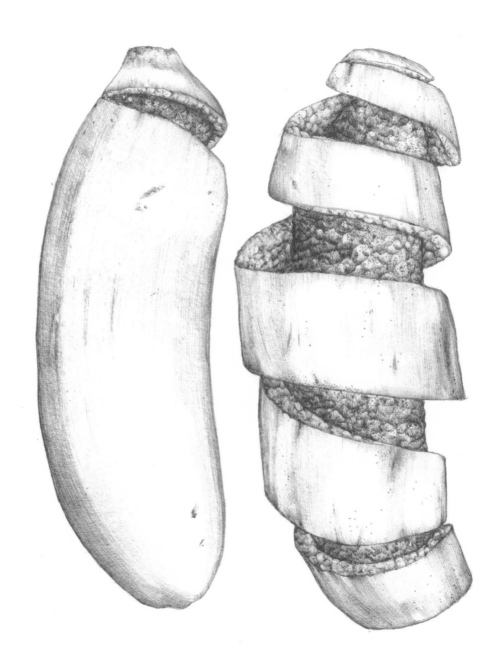

PEELABLE SAUSAGE

Suspiciously similar to a certain yellow fruit, the Peelable Sausage is a handy way to grow and store cultured meat. Fresh from the bioreactor, the sausage is a firm log of muscle tissue safely encased in a bacteria-proof, biodegradable membrane. At this stage, the sausage is ideal for tucking into a hotdog bun, or slicing up and adding to stews. As the sausage ages, it softens and sweetens, taking on a texture akin to a fine tartare. At maximum ripeness, the meat can be squeezed from the casing and used as a sandwich spread. The peel changes color with age so shoppers know if their sausage contains a nice knockwurst or a creamy pâté.

SAUSAGE LUMPIA WITH PEANUT SAUCE

- 4 peelable sausages, extremely ripe
- 1 can of coconut milk
- 60 grams Thai red curry paste
- 180 milliliters peanut butter
- 150 grams sugar
- 2 tablespoons white vinegar
- 1/2 tablespoon salt
- 120 milliliters water
- 8 lumpia wrappers
- Vegetable oil

① Place a steamer inset over a pan of simmering water. Steam the lumpia wrappers for several minutes, until they have softened and are easy to pull apart.

② While the wrappers are steaming, combine the coconut milk, curry paste, peanut butter, sugar, vinegar, salt and water in a saucepan. Bring the mixture to a boil and immediately reduce to a simmer. Simmer for five minutes, stirring frequently. Remove from heat.

③ Remove the sausages from their casing and cut each one in half. Carefully wrap each sausage half with a lumpia wrapper.

④ Pour seven centimeters of oil into a pot, wok or Dutch oven. Heat the oil to 180° C. Fry each peelable sausage for five minutes, until the wrapper is golden brown and crispy. Serve with the peanut sauce for dipping.

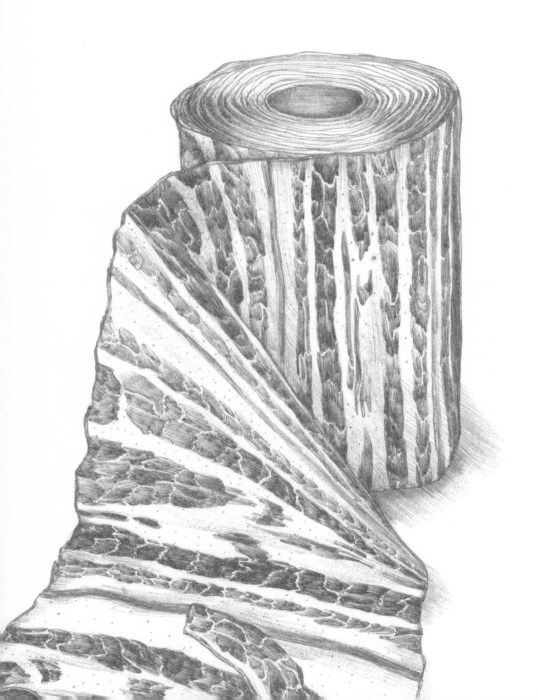

Toilet paper meets bacon for the ultimate convenience food. Snip off slivers to add to a stir-fry. Cut some slices for breakfast. Wrap yourself in bacon and go dressed as a meat mummy for your next costume party. Like all convenience foods, 'muscle tissues' may be on heavy rotation at chain restaurants and hotels. Their consistent size and even distribution of fat and meat is a plus for anyone who needs to churn out large quantities of uniform food. That's not to say that Bacon On A Roll is purely utilitarian: while some rolls use the traditional stripy bacon pattern, others can have the fat printed in cute patterns of frolicking piglets and puppies.

BOXED BACON AND EGG

- 12 square sheets of bacon roll
- 8 eggs
- 1 handful cheddar cheese, shredded
- 1/4 teaspoon black pepper
- 1/4 teaspoon salt

① Preheat the oven to 180° C. Grease the cups in a 12-cup muffin tin.

② Crack the eggs in a bowl and whisk together with the cheddar cheese, salt and pepper.

③ Line each cup in the muffin tin with a sheet of bacon. Divide the egg mixture between the tins. Fold the corners of each bacon sheet inwards to create small boxes. Optional: top each box with a bacon bow.

④ Bake for 30 minutes, or until the eggs have set.

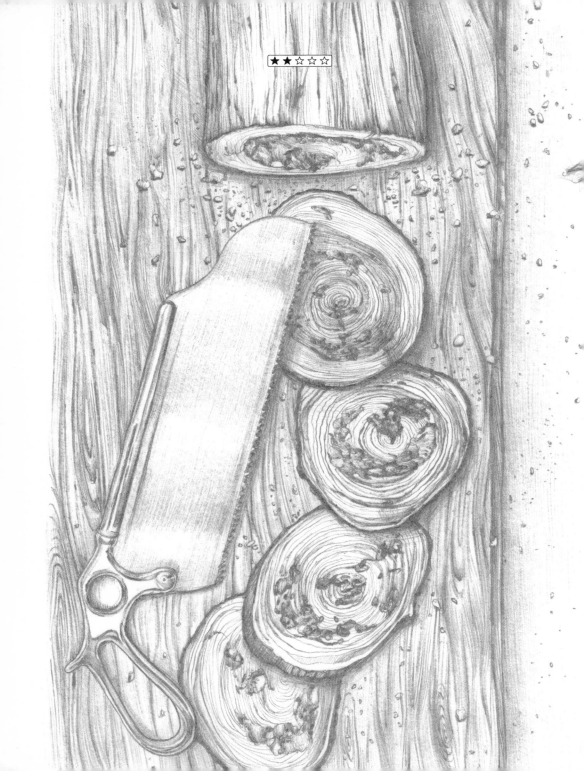

LABCHOPS

Labchops blur the boundaries between logging and butchery. Freshly harvested Labchop 'trunks' arrive by the truckload to in vitro butchers. Armed with bonesaws and hatchets, butchers hack the cultured meat into steaks, planks and roasts. Eagerfoodies will take courses in Labchop butchery to feel a more a natural, visceral connection to lab-grown products.

Put a carnivorous spin on the bûche de Noël by replacing the sweet cake with a meat tree. Or, as in this recipe, bring the (real) forest to the Labchop by slowly smoking a meaty log over maple woodchips. Once the meat is eaten, there's a treat for the patient chef: the bone in the center is filled with succulent marrow. One taste of the juicy, meaty marrow will have you reconsidering your stance on deforestation.

MAPLE SMOKED LABCHOPS

- 3 kilos labchop
- 150 grams dark brown sugar
- 140 grams salt
- 1 tablespoon each garlic powder, onion powder, Spanish paprika, chili powder, cumin and celery salt
- Vegetable oil
- 2 generous handfuls maple wood for smoking

① Mix together the dry ingredients. Rub the labchop with vegetable oil and season generously with the dry mix. Refrigerate for one hour.

② Heat a smoker to 98° C. Smoke the labchop for 10 to 12 hours. The meat is ready when it shreds easily with a fork. When the meat is done, remove it from the smoker, tent with tinfoil, and let rest for an hour.

③ Shred the meat using two forks. To make a labchop sandwich, mix the meat with barbecue sauce, preferably a maple syrup-based sauce, and pile in a split bun or roll. Serve with coleslaw.

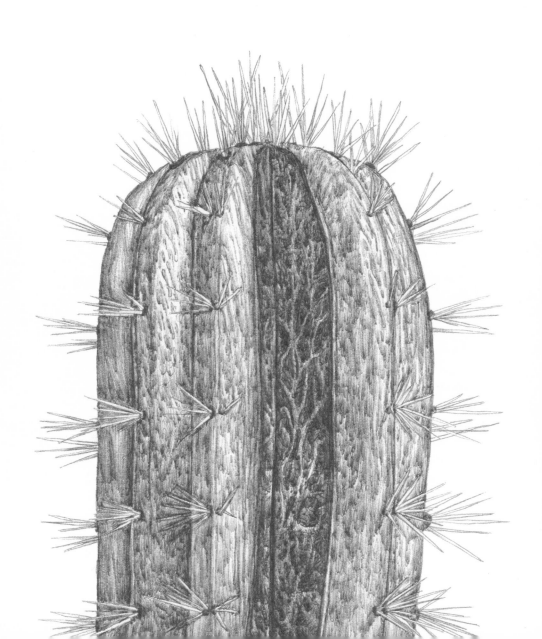

MEAT CACTUS

If in vitro meat becomes the meat production standard, animal ranching becomes a mere historical curiosity. In place of cattle, meat cacti could sprout up in the droughty regions of Argentina, Australia and the United States that were once responsible for much of the world's beef production. The Meat Cactus could be an ideal solution for a world suffering from devastating water shortages.

Unlike cows, meat cacti don't graze, don't emit greenhouse gases, and don't need to be fenced in. These tough, slow-growing succulents are perfectly designed for the harsh environment of the desert. Their thick, leathery skin prevents moisture loss, while a covering of razor-sharp spikes fends off predators like bobcats and coyotes. Hikers lost in the desert could fry up a meal of cactus steak while they wait for rescue.

TACOS WITH 'NOPALES DE CARNE'

- 4 cactus steaks
- 1 corn cob
- Juice from half a lime
- 2 tablespoons cilantro, chopped
- 1/4 white onion, thinly sliced
- 4 small radishes, thinly sliced
- 1 avocado, sliced
- 200 grams of queso fresco or feta cheese, crumbled
- Salt
- Vegetable oil
- Corn tortillas

① Preheat a grill. Brush the cactus with oil and season with a hint of salt.

② Grill the cactus and the corn. Grill the cactus for five minutes on each side. Grill the corn until the kernels are cooked through. Let the cactus cool, then slice into strips. Cut the corn kernels off the cob.

③ In a large bowl, combine the cactus, corn, lime juice and cilantro. Season to taste with salt and pepper. Divide the cactus filling between eight tortillas and garnish with the onion, radish, avocado and cheese.

KNITTED MEAT

While traditional meat cuts refer to the anatomy of the animal — think spare rib, belly slice or T-bone — this is no longer a given with in vitro meat. As a result we can produce meat in any shape our technology and imagination allows us. The knitted meat scenario envisions that 'steaks' will be knitted from thin strains of in vitro meat in any shape and size the customer desires, combining the nostalgia of knitting with the innovative in vitro production technique.

GROWING THE FUTURE OF MEAT

ESSAY BY CHRISTINA AGAPAKIS

Biology grows. In petri dishes or bodies, cells grow and multiply, self-regulating and self-repairing. By taking advantage of the power of biological growth, a single stem cell can theoretically be nurtured to grow indefinitely. Outside of the limits imposed by the edges of an animal's body, the cells can reproduce and multiply until they exhaust the nutrients and space provided, filling petri dishes and vats to grow the future of meat.

Food grows in domesticated plants and animals, but to produce food for a growing population under the rubrics of industrial capitalism, we force biological growth into an unsustainable model where bigger is better — at any cost. Industrial meat production requires huge inputs of energy, water, and land to grow animal feed. Animal wastes create polluting runoff and greenhouse gases. Industrially produced meat is cruel to animals, damaging to the environment, dangerous to workers, and is creating a growing threat to public health through the overuse of antibiotics. Because the costs of such externalities aren't factored into the price of a hamburger at the supermarket, however, this model persists.

In vitro meat is presented as an alternative to factory farming, eliminating troublesome externalities through technological efficiency. Instead of dirty and dangerous slaughterhouses we're shown renderings of the gleaming stainless steel surfaces of a brewing facility, with cells happily growing in vats. Instead of acres of intensively farmed crops we see mockups of ponds of genetically engineered algae, designed to make the perfect mixture of nutrients for growing meat cells. Instead of farms, farmers, cows and their complexities, in vitro meat gives us clean labs, scientists in white coats, and plastic dishes filled with pink liquid.

Today's industry focuses on controlling rather than accommodating growth

Removing animals from the system, in vitro meat abstracts flesh into a collection of cells fed by a bath of nutrients. Advocates for in vitro meat rightly emphasize the externalities of factory farming, making visible costs that most people would prefer to keep hidden. But the abstraction of meat to cells produces and hides new externalities. While in vitro meat grows outside of an animal, it doesn't grow outside of industrial models of food production.

The physicist and writer Ursula Franklin discusses two different industrial models in her manifesto on the social effects of engineering, The Real World of Technology. In the book, Franklin uses biology as a metaphor for the 'growth model', where engineers encourage technologies to grow 'organically', according to the limits of available resources. In contrast, the "production model" that dominates today's industry focuses on controlling rather than accommodating growth. Production models aim to maximize the volume of the product and minimize its price, leaving environmental concerns, health issues, and working conditions aside. The intensive micromanagement and damaging externalities of factory farming are classic features of the production model. Rather than disrupting the production model of factory farming, current visions of in vitro meat take industrial logics to their extremes.

Animals are bred, fed, and given antibiotics to maximize the size of future cuts of meat at the lowest possible price

Tissue engineer Mark Post, a leader in the field, has spoken about the biological inefficiencies that in vitro meat may be able to address. Animals like cows and pigs, he said, weren't designed to efficiently convert vegetable protein into animal protein. Only 15% of the calories fed to farm animals become usable meat calories. In contrast, Post argues that with in vitro meat, "we can control all the variables… and probably can make it much more efficient than the animal can."

What are the variables involved? A steak is the result of a highly coordinated system of cellular growth, where the three dimensional arrangement of bone, cartilage, tendons, fat, muscle, and blood vessels grows with the animal. The animal's digestive system and metabolism turn grass into more cells, and the circulatory system brings nutrients and removes waste. The skin and the immune system protect the meat from infection, and the skeletal system exercises the muscle, creating the tone and texture of the future steak. Factory farming aims to control these biological variables by regulating animal bodies, forcing animals into conditions that optimize speed, size, consistency, and efficiency over environmental safety, human health, and animal welfare. Animals are bred, fed, and given antibiotics to maximize the size of future cuts of meat at the lowest possible price. Factory farms are indeed factories — assembly lines that manufacture living creatures into shrink-wrapped steaks.

With in vitro meat, cells are warmed, nourished, cleaned, and exercised using only complex machinery

With in vitro meat, the dream of the meat assembly line reaches a logical conclusion: cells are warmed, nourished, cleaned, and exercised using only complex machinery. Tissues are formed by the controlled placement of cells in a 3D printer. Cuts of meat are designed, flavored, and packaged by a series of imagined devices. In vitro meat will be made, not grown.

While attempting to control all the variables of biological growth, the designers of these machines conceal the real labor and resources that must go in to make meat in vitro. To survive and grow in culture, cells not only need sugars, fats, proteins, vitamins, and minerals, but also a set of hormones and growth factors that stimulate the cells to divide outside the context of a body. Currently, these factors are provided by supplementing the nutrient broth with fetal bovine serum drained from unborn calves after pregnant cows go to slaughter.

The fact that in vitro meat depends directly on the byproducts of current industrial meat production, however, is routinely left out of the narratives of progress and 'cruelty free' meat.

Likewise, we hear about the antibiotics used in factory farming, but almost never the fact that without an immune system, cells in culture must be protected by large quantities of antibiotics and fungicides. We hear about the costs of growing corn in monoculture to produce animal feed, but we don't hear about the refined sugars and amino acids that cells need in vitro, or where they come from, besides vague references to engineered algae. These are a different kind of externality, hidden from view not because of the economics of in vitro meat, which are not yet in place, but because of the philosophy of industrial control.

The usual response to such critiques is that these problems will be solved by the inevitable march of technological progress. However, it is precisely these incompletenesses — problems not yet solved — that persist and plague the production model. As Franklin writes, the production model assumes that production happens "under conditions that are, at least in principle, entirely controllable. If in practice such control is not complete or completely successful, then there is an assumption, implicit in the model itself, that improvements in knowledge, design, and organization can occur so that all essential parameters will become controllable." In the aggressive pursuit of efficiency and profit margins, the easiest way to solve these problems is to banish them out of the frame (as with factory farming) or to the future (as with in vitro meat).

Advocates of in vitro meat — and perhaps readers of this essay — may see in my criticism a wish to 'return to nature', to reverse technological progress and throw us all into a life of agrarian serfdom. But a critique of this particular technology is not the same as arguing against all technology. Seeing criticism of in vitro meat as anti-technology relies on the assumption that technology is only one thing, that it has a singular path, and that in vitro meat is already inevitable. This kind of argument is intended to shut down reasoned debate, closing off discussion of how technologies come into existence and work in the real world in favor of a blind faith that in the future, we will inevitably control all the variables.

Biology can be sustainable, adapting and growing within environmental, social and economic contexts

Food lies at the complex intersection of biology, technology, and culture. There is no single technology that can address all these complexities, and there will always be variables that escape our grasp. No single technology will 'feed the world'. To build a sustainable growth model for producing food in the future, we will use many old technologies alongside new technologies that have not yet been invented. We will design technologies that help grow foods according to local environments and cultures, enriching soils with diverse populations of microorganisms, recycling wastes and distributing food more equitably. For meat eating, this will mean working to incorporate animals back into diverse systems of agriculture rather than separating them in factory farms, and importantly, it will likely mean eating a lot less meat. Accomplishing these goals will not come easy, and will require a fundamental shift in how we understand and regulate the ways we produce food. Biology can be sustainable, adapting and growing within environmental, social, and economic contexts, but as long as we focus only on industrial efficiencies and hyper-technological dreams, we won't be able to grow out of the production model.

Now that we've started mastering the practicalities of producing in vitro meat, it's time to play with our food. Besides being perfectly pathogen-free, in vitro meat could be grow in nearly any shape, size or species. From cannibal clubs to meat foam cocktail bars, fantastic new food cultures might spring up in response to emerging technologies. At the same time, it's important not to lose contact with the past. Chefs and scientists could adapt artisanal meat production for an in vitro age. The care our great-grandparents devoted to raising their livestock could be a model for our own behavior as we are moving towards a brave new world of meat.

Based on the Chinese art of 'flowering tea', Meat Flowers are sold as small, tightly wrapped bundles of in vitro meat. Only when placed in hot liquid the round bundles magically unfurl into elaborate flowers, complete with delicate leaves and petals. Intricate designs such as chrysanthemums or lilies can take skilled meat artisans up to 15 minutes to assemble and sew.

So their intricate artistry can be admired from all angles, these flowers are best used in clear soup stock and served in glass containers. In the following recipe, a meat flower 'blooms' in a Vietnamese broth garnished with a garden of fragrant Asian herbs.

FLOWERING PHO

- 1 liter pho broth
- 2 meat flowers
- 250 grams dried flat rice noodles
- 2 scallions, thinly sliced
- 1 small onion, thinly sliced
- 1 chili pepper, sliced
- 1 lime, cut into wedges
- Handful each of bean sprouts, cilantro and Thai basil
- Hoisin sauce
- Sriracha sauce

① Bring the broth to a simmer.

② While the broth is simmering, cover the noodles with hot water and let stand for 30 minutes, until tender but not mushy. Drain the noodles.

③ Divide the noodles and broth into two bowls. Add the onion, scallions, chili, bean sprouts and herbs to each bowl, arranging the garnishes in attractive groupings. Place a meat flower into each bowl immediately before serving. Add hoisin sauce, Sriracha sauce and lime juice to taste.

ORIGAMI MEAT

Lab-grown meat is often cultured in sheets only a few cells thick. The art of Origami Meat takes advantage of these paper-like properties to craft flowers and animals folded from beef, pork or more exotic meats.

An ancient Japanese legend holds that anyone who folds 1,000 origami cranes will be granted a wish by a mystical crane, a benevolent creature said to live for a 1,000 years. Now, equally long-lived lines of red-crowned crane cells could be cultured for Origami Meat, allowing the hopeful to fold origami cranes from real crane meat, doubling the auspicious elements of this practice. A feast of 1,000 cranes could be a perfect hors d'oeuvre for a wedding or major gala.

1000 CRANE FEAST

- 1000 origami meat cranes
- 500 milliliters vegetable oil
- 10 heads of garlic, minced
- 1 liter white miso paste
- 1 liter apricot jam
- 500 milliliters rice vinegar
- 500 milliliters water

① Preheat an oven to 220° C. Set the shape of origami meat cranes by using a chef's blow torch to briefly cook the folds in the meat. Refrigerate the cranes on baking sheets.

② In a very large pan, heat the oil over medium heat. Add the garlic and cook until fragrant. Add the miso, jam, vinegar and water. Whisk until smooth. Bring the mixture to a boil, whisking frequently, then remove the pan from the heat.

③ Brush each crane with the glaze. Bake in the oven for three minutes. Remove from the oven, brush again with glaze, then bake for an additional three minutes, or until the meat is browned on the edges and cooked through in the center.

Meat Fruit seduces diners with an entirely new eating experience that melds vegetarian and carnivorous traditions. Inspired by medieval dishes that fashioned fake fruit from real meat, Meat Fruit grows muscle tissue with a cellular structure that precisely mimics that of berries, oranges, or mangoes. Meat Fruit combines the femininity of fruit with the masculine sensibilities of red meat in a hybrid celebration of our post-patriarchal, post-gender society.

Meat Fruit lends itself to surprising combinations, such as in these tartlets that replace crème pâtissière with savory custard. Meat fruit 'berries' are a savory-sweet amuse that begins with an intense hit of beef and finishes with the tart tones of forest berries.

MEAT FRUIT TARTLETS

- 500 grams flour
- 250 grams cold butter, cubed
- 480 milliliters cream
- 1/2 teaspoon salt
- 3 eggs, divided
- 2 egg yolks
- 100 grams goat cheese
- 400 grams meat fruit
- Fig jam, diluted with water

① In a bowl, mix the flour and butter with your fingers until the mixture resembles breadcrumbs. Beat one egg and add to the flour. Mix until a dough forms. Refrigerate for 10 minutes.

② Preheat the oven to 180° C. On a floured surface, roll out the dough to a 5 millimeter thickness. Cut the dough with a 10 centimeter round cutter. Line miniature tart tins with the pastry and bake for 15 minutes.

③ Whisk salt, egg yolks, and two eggs in a bowl. Heat the cream and goat cheese in a saucepan, whisking until the cheese has melted. Dribble the cream mixture into the eggs, whisking continuously. Pour the custard into the pastry shells. Bake at 150° C for 25 minutes.

④ Remove the tartlets from the oven and let cool. Top each with meat fruit and brush with a thin layer of jam.

CARNERY BREWPUB

Beer is made in breweries, wine is made in wineries, and meat could be made in carneries. 'Carniculture' ranges in size from enormous commercial facilities to countertop bioreactors. Situated between the industrial and the personal, brewpubs may find particular resonance in the brewing of beer and the growing of in vitro meat. These self-consciously 'vintage' spots can offer homegrown versions of heritage meats and microbrewed lagers and stouts. Sitting on chairs upholstered with rich in vitro leather, diners could sample in vitro charcuterie plates alongside flights of the house beers. Lit by the gentle green glow from illuminated algae tanks, old-fashioned copper beer tanks may be complimented by the modern look of stainless steel bioreactors.

BEER AND BREWED MEAT PAIRING

- 3 to 5 varieties of beer
- 3 to 5 varieties of cured in vitro meat
- 1 baguette, thinly sliced
- Wholegrain mustard
- Cornichon pickles
- Olives

① Place the mustard, cornichons, and olives in small bowls. Put the sliced baguette on a plate.

② Serve each beer with an accompanying meat. There are no hard-and-fast rules for meat and beer pairing, though it's best to pair beers and meats with similar flavor profiles. Lighter beers such as Kölsch, white beer and pale ale go well with cervelat, pancetta, or mortadella. Darker beers such as stout are best served with stronger meats such as smoked turkey, venison or andouille sausage.

MEAT FETISHISM

In vitro meat can be offered in an unbelievable variety of shapes, flavors, colors and textures — you'd have to eat for years to get your fill of every kind. Overwhelmed with such a diversity of cultured flesh, some meat-lovers could turn into bona fide Meat Fetishists.

These hardcore carnivores may transform once-vegetarian foods into pure, lab-grown meat. Proclaiming the health benefits of an exclusively carnivorous lifestyle, these purists make salads with meat lettuce, sandwiches with meat bread, and even carve their Halloween pumpkins from squash-shaped lumps of meat. Meat Fetishists, young and old alike, will abandon 'real' vegetables in favor of 100% meat replacements.

MEAT FETISH MEAL

- 400 milliliters ketchup
- 60 milliliters cider vinegar
- 60 milliliters Worcestershire sauce
- 50 grams brown sugar
- 2 tablespoons molasses
- 2 tablespoons yellow mustard
- 1 tablespoon Tabasco sauce
- 1/2 teaspoon black pepper
- 4 labchops
- 400 grams meat peas
- 400 grams meat potatoes
- 200 grams meat mushrooms
- 2 tablespoons vegetable oil

① Combine the first eight ingredients in a saucepan. Bring to a boil. Reduce the heat to a simmer and cook the sauce for 15 minutes.

② Using a food processor, grind the meat potatoes into a paste-like consistency. Chill in the refrigerator.

③ In a skillet, heat one tablespoon of oil until shimmering. Add the meat peas and meat mushrooms and cook until no longer raw in the center.

④ Heat the additional oil in the skillet. Cook the labchops for four minutes, flip, and cook an additional four minutes, until the outside is well browned but the center is medium-rare. Serve the chops, peas, mushrooms and mashed potatoes with a generous drizzle of sauce.

MEAT COCKTAIL

What's better than warm, comforting soup? Comforting soup that gets you drunk. The advent of in vitro meat may prove irresistible to experimental bartenders who could take the savory cocktail trend to its logical extreme. No animal will be off limit as mixologists infuse, foam and shake their way to Margaritaville, population: meat.

A meat-based riff on the classic White Russian cocktail, the Liquid Turducken combines turkey, duck and chicken into a hearty drink that's practically a meal in itself. While plenty of pre-infused spirits are available for purchase, it's far more satisfying to infuse meat into your drink at home. Experiment with adding bacon to bourbon, for instance, or whale meat to saké.

LIQUID TURDUCKEN

- 250 grams roast in vitro chicken, shredded
- 250 grams roast in vitro duck, shredded
- 1 liter of vodka
- 500 milliliters milk
- 1 liter turkey stock, salted to taste

① Add the milk and duck to a medium saucepan. Heat the milk to a gentle simmer, then immediately remove from the heat. Transfer to a container, cover, and chill overnight. The next day, strain the solids from the milk using a coffee filter or cheesecloth.

② Add the vodka and chicken to a mason jar or other tightly sealed container. Chill in the freezer overnight, preferably longer, until the vodka develops a strong chicken flavor.

③ To make a single cocktail: Using a pipette, pipe 30 milliliters of the duck milk into a tall glass. Taking care not to disturb the first layer, pipe in 20 milliliters of the turkey stock. Finish the cocktail by piping in 50 milliliters of the roast chicken vodka. The differing densities of the liquids will keep the layers separate; it's up to the drinker to stir them together.

IN VITRO ICE CREAM

For most people in the Western world, eating food right out of the freezer means only one thing: time for dessert. But why limit sorbet and ice cream to the end of the meal? In many parts of Asia, diners have no qualms about scooping up savory-sweet frozen treats made with corn, prawn and roast beef. In Vitro Ice Cream blends the velvety mouthfeel of ice cream with the taste of popular meats like fried chicken and smoked ham. Not content to only reproduce standard meats, In Vitro Ice Cream comes in a whole truck's worth of out-there flavors. 'Dragon' is a fire-breathing blend of meat that tastes just like a mythological beast, while 'polar bear' is salty, snowy and cultured from an actual bear.

FRIED CHICKEN ICE CREAM SUNDAE

- 1 liter chicken ice cream
- 1 liter cornflakes, crushed
- 240 milliliters potato chips, crushed
- 1/2 teaspoon salt
- 2 eggs
- 1 tablespoon milk
- Whipped mashed potatoes
- Gravy
- Peanut or vegetable oil for frying

① Scoop out round balls of chicken ice cream and place on a parchment-lined baking sheet. Freeze the balls for two hours, until they are very hard.

② Mix the cornflakes and potato chips together in a bowl. Roll the balls of ice cream in this mixture, then freeze for 30 minutes.

③ Whisk together the eggs, milk and salt. Roll each ball in the egg mixture, then the cornflake mixture. Freeze for two hours.

④ Pour seven centimeters of oil into a pot, wok, or Dutch oven. Heat the oil to 200° C. Working in batches, carefully drop each ball into the oil. Cook the balls for 30 seconds, until golden brown. Drain on a paper towel. Serve with a scoop of mashed potatoes and a drizzle of gravy.

MEAT PAINT

Meat Paint is just like normal paint — except it's safe to eat and completely delicious. Kids love doodling on baking sheets with the colorful squeeze-tubes of lab-grown meat. The completed artwork is baked in the oven for a one-of-a-kind treat. Meat Paint is a fantastic way to get your children excited about cooking.

All sets of Meat Paint come with baking paper printed with paint-by-numbers scenes. However, true artists love to go freeform and 'paint' a landscape of meat and roast vegetables. It's a great way to persuade picky eaters to try in vitro meat and unfamiliar veggies. Meat Paint goes great with anything that's baked or roasted, so try it squiggled on bread, potatoes, or whole in vitro hams.

LANDSCAPE MEAT PAINTING

- Meat paint
- A selection of vegetables suitable for roasting: asparagus, broccoli, potatoes, tomatoes, carrots, parsnips, leeks, onions, or fennel.
- 60 milliliters olive oil
- 60 milliliters balsamic vinegar
- Salt and pepper

① Preheat the oven to 230° C. Whisk the olive oil and balsamic vinegar together in a bowl.

② On a baking sheet lined with parchment paper, assemble the meat painting. Paint a scene of a blue meat sea afloat with carrot goldfish and tomato beach balls, or invent a landscape with asparagus grass and a big yellow in vitro sun.

③ Brush the vegetables with the oil and vinegar mixture. Season the entire tray with salt and pepper. Bake for 35 to 45 minutes.

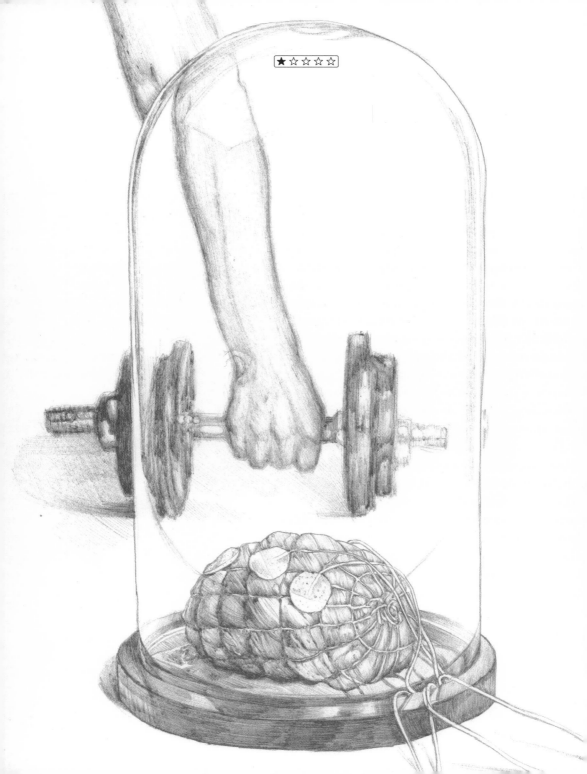

The Muscle Mass Roast is the ultimate workout companion for weightlifters and body builders. Linked by an internet connection to a special scale, the muscle mass roast gains muscle at the same rate you do. The bigger and bulkier you get, the more meat your muscle mass grows. There's no better way to stay motivated at the gym than knowing your hard work will translate into a muscular steak.

Surprise your friends with your new body, not to mention your new culinary skills. Can your muscle gain feed four people? Ten? Twenty? In this recipe, there's no better way to prove your manliness — or womanliness — by braising the evidence of your workout success in a tough, masculine mixture of bourbon and beer.

BEER AND BOURBON BRAISED MUSCLE MASS

- 2 kilos of muscle mass roast
- 2 tablespoons vegetable oil
- 1 medium onion, chopped
- 3 cloves of garlic, minced
- 1 liter beef broth
- 1 bottle dark beer
- 180 milliliters bourbon
- 50 grams brown sugar
- 60 milliliters soy sauce
- 3 celery stalks, chopped
- 2 tomatoes, chopped
- 1 carrot, chopped
- 1 tablespoon balsamic vinegar

① Preheat the oven to 160° C. Heat one tablespoon of oil in a large pot. Add the muscle mass and cook, without moving, until one side is well-browned. Repeat on the second side. Transfer the meat to a plate.

② Heat the remaining oil. Add the onion and garlic and cook for five minutes. Add the broth and remaining ingredients. Bring to a simmer.

③ Return the meat to the pot, cover, and transfer to the oven. Roast for 5 hours, until very tender but not falling apart. Transfer the meat to a plate. Strain the remaining liquid, return it to the pot, and simmer for 15 minutes. Serve the meat sliced against the grain with the liquid spooned on top.

CELEBRITY CUBES

Forget autographs or posters. Prove that you're the ultimate fan of a celebrity by eating him or her. Celebrity Cubes have turned the stem cells from some of today's biggest stars into a range of tasty meats. Give European royalty a try before the next coronation, or go pop-culture by frying up the flesh from each member of a boy band. If you can't be famous, you can at least eat famous.

What better way to serve a celebrity than bathed in an addictive whiskey glaze? Popstars might have to go to rehab after too much boozing, but this recipe is guaranteed to make it safely to your plate, no driving under influence or arrests necessary.

WHISKEY-GLAZED CELEBRITY CUBES

- 120 milliliters whiskey
- 120 milliliters apple cider
- 2 tablespoons light brown sugar
- 4 teaspoons cider vinegar
- 1 tablespoon Dijon mustard
- 1/4 teaspoon cayenne pepper
- 1 kilo celebrity cubes, any individual
- 1 tablespoon vegetable oil
- Salt and pepper
- 1 tablespoon unsalted butter

① Whisk the first six ingredients together in a bowl. In a resealable plastic bag, mix the celebrity cubes and 60 milliliters of the whiskey mixture. Refrigerate for two hours.

② Remove the celebrity cubes from the bag. Heat the oil in a skillet until just beginning to smoke. Season the cubes with salt and pepper and cook until browned on all sides. Transfer the cubes to a plate and cover with aluminum foil.

③ Add the remaining whiskey mixture to the pan and bring to a boil. Cook for three to five minutes. Add the butter and simmer for another three minutes.

④ Return the cubes to the pan, turning to coat. Cook until an instant-read thermometer inserted in the center of a cube reads 60° C. Serve the celebrity cubes with the remaining sauce.

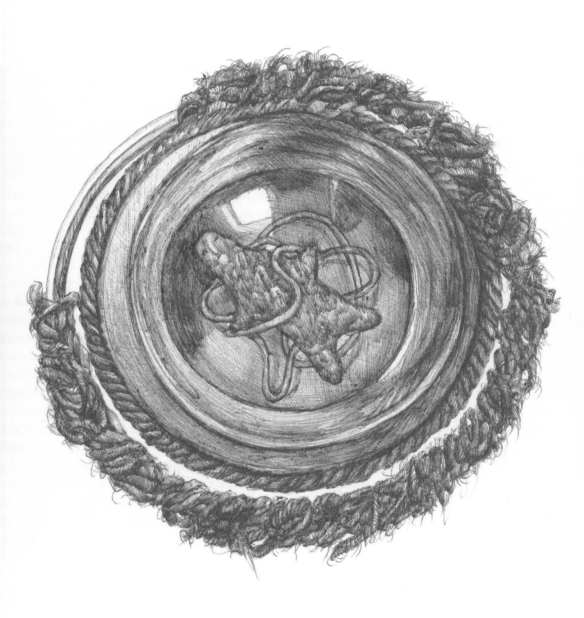

In Vitro Me is a personal bioreactor worn as a pendent nestled between the collarbones. Over the course of several months, a small effigy cultured from your own stem cells will grow within the bioreactor. Because the muscle tissue is fed by your own blood supply, diet and emotion play a key role in the final flavor of each in vitro me.

In this recipe, the porky flavor of human flesh is complimented with a blood-red glaze that lends sensuous notes of earth, sugar and smoke. A more modern, gentler update on centuries-old cannibal rituals, In Vitro Me is best shared with a lover as the ultimate expression of unity.

IN VITRO US

- 2 in vitro me effigies
- 60 grams butter
- A pinch each of salt, pepper, and chipotle powder
- 90 milliliters maple syrup
- 90 milliliters broth
- 1 small beet, peeled and diced
- 30 ml Worcestershire sauce
- Begonia blossoms

① Preheat the oven to 180° C. Combine the maple syrup, broth and beet in a saucepan and bring to a boil. Lower heat and simmer until the glaze has been reduced by half.

② Melt the butter in a heavy skillet. Add the meat and cook until browned, one to two minutes per side. Transfer the meat to a small baking dish. Pour the glaze over the meat, turning to coat. Bake for eight to ten minutes, until an instant-read thermometer inserted in the center reads 57° C.

③ Remove the meat from the baking dish, put on two serving plates and cover with aluminum foil. Return the glaze to the saucepan, and simmer until it is think and syrupy. Using an immersion blender, blend the glaze until no beet chunks remain.

④ Drizzle the glaze over the in vitro me and garnish with the blossoms.

THE CARNERY

Although in vitro meat technology
is typically perceived as a high-tech
and futuristic product, the cultivation
of cell cultures stands in a long tradition
of beer brewing and cheese making.
Such existing practices could be of
inspiration for the future of in vitro meat.
One day, growing meat may be as natural
as making cheese or beer. Like todays
brewpubs, the carnery could become an
artesian way of growing meat in cities,
or even in restaurants.

THE CARNERY

ESSAY BY ISHA DATAR AND ROBERT BOLTON

Imagine London 2025. The first in vitro carnery 'Counter Culture' opens its doors. The restored 1970s-era English brewpub boasts an expansive bar of reclaimed mahogany and booths upholstered with magnificent in vitro leather. Steaks are grown to precision inside giant steel vats, decorated (functionally) with illuminated green algae tanks. A disorienting mingling of global spices flavor varieties of exotic and heritage meats like boar and Berkshire, all of which are cultured on site. The large charcuterie board, consisting of mushroom-media duck foie gras, coriander mortadella and crispy lobes of sweetbread pairs perfectly with a shortlist of probiotic cocktails (try the rum and kombucha).

In vitro meat has the capacity to transform meat production as we know it, not only offering new and diverse types of product but also introducing an entirely new way of thinking about and interacting with food. One day, growing meat may seem as natural as making cheese or beer.

The farm was long the cultural ground connecting humans to our food and to our labor. Through over 10,000 years of agricultural practice, farming — food and work — was a foundation on which we developed our sense of humanity. From values like integrity, quality, respect and stewardship, to experiences of shared knowledge and enjoyment, to developing our relationship with land and species and gaining a concept of the cyclical passage of time that connects us to the seasons – the farm has been our cultural rooting. Keeping farm animals played an integral role in maintaining the farm. Animal husbandry and crop cultivation were concerted activities. Animals were fed on crop residues after a crop was harvested, or on pastures that were unfit for farming. Manure was used to replenish soils. Animals were slaughtered and shared. Meat was honored and savored.

One day, growing meat may seem as natural as making cheese or beer

The farm has also been a locus of human innovation. To meet and exceed consumer demands for food, the farm has been a site of cutting edge breakthroughs in mechanical engineering, genetics, and chemistry. The craft of tending the herd evolved into processes of automation and directives. Meat production scaled to a point where it can no longer fit into a cyclical and sustainable farming system. Today the majority of meat is produced on industrial farms, where animals are bred, raised and slaughtered for the principal purpose of producing food for human beings. Crops that could feed humans are instead fed to meat animals. Fertilizer is produced in such quantities that it spoils soils rather than nourishing them. In many ways animals are treated as living meat-producing bioreactors with human food as an input, polluting waste as an output, and various drugs, hormones, and genetic manipulations added to make the process more 'efficient'. Price is the defining product characteristic and minimizing this incurs vast external costs to the environment, animal welfare, and public health.

Further, meat is defined as a small handful of species, presented by a smaller handful of corporations. Few players, little product diversity, and a very narrow, inexpensive price range characterize the meat production industry status quo. In light of population increase, food insecurity, volatile food prices, environmental concerns and changing value systems around food — it is clear that current modes of production cannot persist. For meat production to take place responsibly, we will have to significantly diversify our eating habits, and with them, our production habits. In vitro meat is one promising alternative. We don't know enough about it yet. But we know we can make it. And we are responsible for exploring what it will mean not only for our health and environment, but also for our culture, and our sense of humanity. How should we feel about interacting with lab-grown meat?

If we're comfortable treating meat animals like bioreactors, and engineering them strictly for the purpose of maximal protein production — then perhaps we can go a step further. Meat is simply a collection of muscle, fat and connective tissues. Rather than raise an entire complex organism only to harvest these tissues, why not start at the basic unit of life, the cell, to produce meat? In vitro meat is meat, created in a bioreactor, rather than in an animal.

A few things are required for making meat in vitro: a cell line, a media to feed the cells, a bioreactor where cell growth can take place, and a structure upon which the cells can attach and grow. Each of these elements allows for limitless variations of technique and process. The room for deviation bridges science with craft, enabling in vitro meat makers to create unique products with unique characteristics and features. At the fictional in vitro meat restaurant Counter Culture that begins this essay, the boar meat could be made with adult stem cells collected from wild boar, cultured in an algae media. Grown in a rotating wall bioreactor on a tubular scaffold, the cell stretches to produce a lean, grained meat. The mushroom media duck foie gras could be made from a co-culture of duck fat and liver cells in a mushroom-based media, 3D printed into a bioabsorbable scaffold to produce a fatty, smooth, and cruelty-free foie gras. The flexibility of in vitro meat production can change and diversify the ways people consume and interact with their food.

In vitro meat is simply meat created outside of the animal

As it stands today, a thick interface separates the experience of eating from the process of food production. Industrial farms are located far from the eyes of consumers and knowledge of what occurs in these farms is limited in the wider public. While consumers are mostly disconnected from the realities of where their food comes from, marketers continue to romanticize the ideal farm of yore, substituting images of agriculture in place of ones of industry, dropping visual cues to the rural farm on packaging, advertising and in retail displays. These signifiers remind us of the core human values and sense of community that we've historically associated with the farm. Indeed, when done well, you can taste the crafted freshness. In the eyes of diners and marketers alike, the distinction between fantasy and reality is apparently trivial, if not entirely non-existent. We buy into rustic theaters of 'artisanal', 'smallbatch' and 'handcrafted' cuisine though the associations we have with these words may bear no resemblance to the actual back-end production processes. The theater of branding is effective enough that we're relieved of our responsibility to confront the truths of our food. In vitro meat may play into this theater — fitting among the existing symbols, textures and cues that make us comfortable with artifice — while breaking down its fourth wall, chipping away the layers, so that like the farmer, the baker, the butcher, and the brewer, we can interface directly with the realities of food production, or making.

Like a bakery where bread is made and a brewery where beer is made, the 'carnery' is where in vitro meat is made

The science and art of culturing cells to produce meat has been called 'carniculture'. Like a bakery where bread is made, a winery where wine is made and a brewery where beer is made, the 'carnery' is where in vitro meat is made. Carniculture might be dressed with similar connotations and aesthetics to the craft brew and farm-to-table movements.

We have to ask not only how in vitro meat products nourish our bodies, but how the process of making them nourishes human culture and fits in with our sense of a modern humanity. How, going forward, can the manufacturer of in vitro meat achieve the symbolic status of the farmer, the baker, and the small batch brewer? How can the carnery, like the bakery, the winery, or the brewery, become an impetus for human culture? Though it uses mammalian cell cultures rather than yeast cultures, a carnery has the potential to look very similar to these facilities — beer breweries in particular.

At the carnery of the future, large stainless steel tanks house the biological processes that are transforming organic ingredients into food products. Conditions like temperature and pressure are controlled and manipulated. Inputs and outputs are carefully measured. The work environment is clean and safe. But it doesn't feel like sterile science. It feels crafted, artisanal — because it is.

As with beer, the basic production scheme for producing in vitro meat can be modified and adapted in endless ways to make products that vary in appearance, aroma, taste, and mouthfeel. This makes for an industry comprised of many diverse products and players, and production on many different scales. A brewery can be massive with several stories-tall bioreactors, located near city limits, or it can be smaller and situated in urban areas. A brewpub restaurant may choose to brew seasonal offerings in-house, while a DIY enthusiast may wish to try his or her hand at making the ultimate personalized brew with a home brewing operation.

Imagine that within the stainless steel tanks at a brewery, microbrewery, brewpub or basement, meat rather than beer, is being brewed. Low cost, mass produced meat is cultured in massive carneries in rural areas. Because the risk of bacterial contamination and viral epidemics is far decreased without the use of animals, the meat production business is no longer at risk of recalls, workers are no longer at risk of health issues, and the local rural environment is no longer at risk of water and air pollution.

Mid-range in vitro meat is made in local carneries in urban areas. These carneries host school and travel tours, educating the public on the art and science of carniculture. Because growing meat in vitro does not require the large tracts of land that factory farms require, this carnery is located in a skyscraper that once contained office space. Algae tanks surround the outer surface of the tower, reaping the unshaded sun available several stories up from ground level.

In contrast to industrial farming, meat production methods go from secretive to celebrated

High priced meats are 'micro-cultured' in trendy neighborhoods at boutique carnery pubs like the fictional Counter Culture described at the beginning of this essay. These small batch facilities create various seasonal offerings, depending on which media ingredients are available and which cell cultures and nutrient profiles are in vogue. Forward thinking restaurants offer signature meats cultured in house, paired with a house wine. Some chefs focus on nutrition profiles, some focus on traditional 'heritage breed' lines and others focus on biomolecular gastronomy. They test the limits of carniculture by culturing rare or extinct species, co-culturing multiple cell types or developing unique never-before-seen cell lines.

Communities of home carniculturists, who began as foodies and DIYbio enthusiasts, swap techniques and recipes at cultured meat cook-offs, fairs, and night markets. Carniculture bloggers post photography, data, and other media documenting their materials, methods and meals online. The home carnery movement spawns carniculture specialty shops, cell culture babysitting services, protocol-swapping websites, cell banks and special interest magazines. Hobbyists seeking to turn their passion into a profession have a variety of certification and apprenticeship programs to choose from to help them join a major carnery or start one of their own.

The in vitro meat industry can become more diverse, responsible, and viable than the current meat industry

In contrast to industrial farming, meat production methods go from secretive to celebrated. Meat production facilities go from vast to vertical. The meat production industry moves from the hands of few to the hands of many. And people grow more authentically connected to the origins and creation stories of what they eat.

For this new industry to exist, some conditions have to be met in the early days of discovery and development. The science has to remain fairly open, transparent, and publicly accessible. With a population of scientists scattered about the planet interested in making in vitro meat a reality, an 'open source' approach to in vitro meat will accelerate development of the technology. Intellectual property protection has a place in the industry at some point, but heavy, prohibitive patent protection early on could stunt this new industry before it has a chance to flourish. Culturing in vitro meat involves a level of 'art' and technique that only comes with experience and familiarity with processes and materials. As such, patent protection will be complemented by trade secrets, secret recipes and the carniculturist's distinct artistry and prowess.

Development needs to coincide with public conversation about meat, meat production, carniculture, and food science. Consumers need and want to know about the origins of their food. The new science of carniculture must be developed responsibly, driven by discourse from the beginning. This is much more likely to happen if research is funded and conducted publicly, openly engaging researchers, DIYbio enthusiasts and students to address scientific hurdles. Creating a food politic that tackles resource use, the environment, public health and animal welfare should be a cooperative movement.

In vitro meat is simply meat created outside of the animal. Cultured meat and carcass meat are the same product, though created through different processes. The potential for carniculture to introduce a more humane and sustainable meat industry is undeniably compelling. With the right set of conditions in place during the development of cultured meat science, carniculture can reduce the need for, or entirely displace factory farming. By embracing transparency and creating a culinary attitude, the in vitro meat industry can become more diverse, responsible, and viable than the current meat industry. A new set of food values emerge, unique from, yet akin to those we associate with the family farm. A future with in vitro meat is indeed a cultured future.

BEFORE WE CAN
DECIDE IF WE WANT TO
EAT MEAT FROM THE
LABORATORY,
WE WILL HAVE TO
EXPLORE THE FOOD
CULTURE IT WILL
BRING US

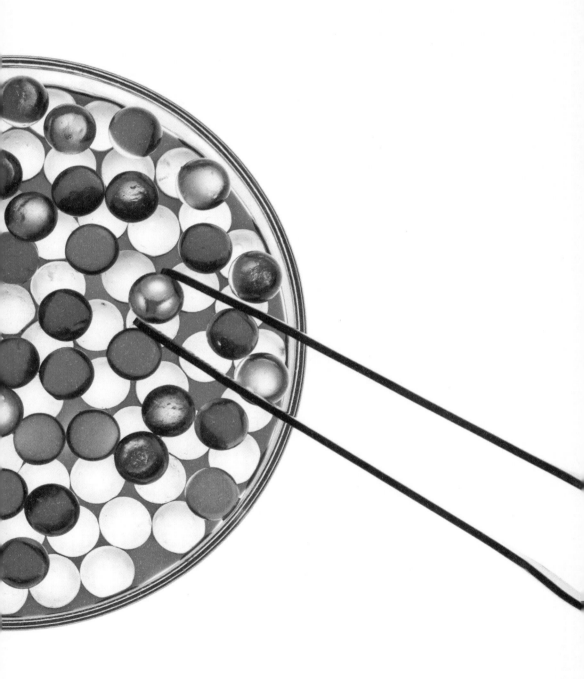

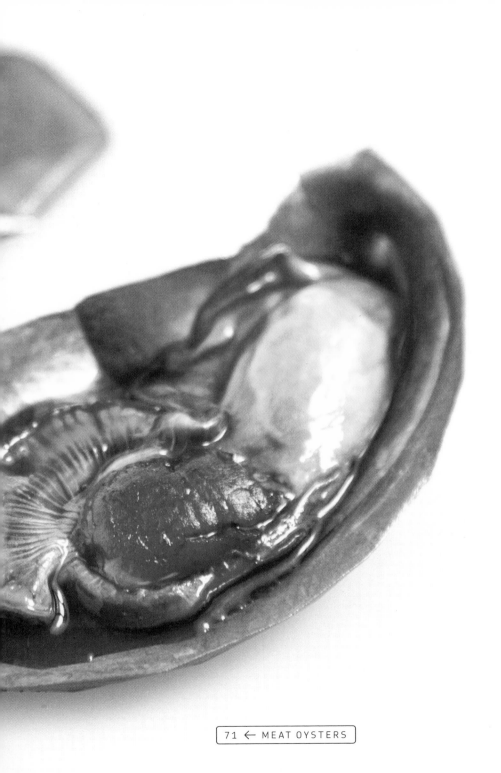